The American Hero in
Children's Literature

The American Hero in Children's Literature

A Standards-Based Approach

Carol M. Butzow
and
John W. Butzow

Teacher Ideas Press, an imprint of Libraries Unlimited
Westport, Connecticut • London

Library of Congress Cataloging-in-Publication Data

Butzow, Carol M., 1942–
    The American hero in children's literature : a standards-based approach / by Carol M.
Butzow and John W. Butzow.
        p. cm.
    Includes index.
    ISBN 1–59469–004–9 (pbk.)
    1. Children's literature, American—Study and teaching.   2. Heroes in literature—Study and
teaching—United States.   3. United States—Biography—Study and teaching.   4.
Children—Books and reading—United States.   I. Butzow, John W., 1939–   II. Title.
PS490.B87   2005
810.9'352—dc22   2005047482

British Library Cataloguing in Publication Data is available.

Library of Congress Catalog Card Number: 2005047482
ISBN: 1–59469–004–9

First published in 2005

Libraries Unlimited/Teacher Ideas Press, 88 Post Road West, Westport, CT 06881
A Member of the Greenwood Publishing Group, Inc.
www.lu.com

Printed in the United States of America

The paper used in this book complies with the
Permanent Paper Standard issued by the National
Information Standards Organization (Z39.48–1984).

10   9   8   7   6   5   4   3   2   1

This work is dedicated to all of the potential heroes in your classroom and to you as you become the instrument of their imagination and development.

Contents

Preface

Every generation has its heroes. Some of these men and women enjoy only a fleeting moment of fame. Others will be assured of a place in history that will override a specific time frame. Heroes are persons who have devoted their lives to the bettering of humanity. They have asked questions for which only they had answers. They have left a lasting mark on society. Above all, they have become role models for those who value and appreciate their contributions to the world.

Children need heroes whom they can look to as role models—as someone who has made the long journey to his or her goal in life, and whose personal accomplishments can be a guide to others. This book, *The American Hero in Children's Literature: A Standards-Based Approach*, is aimed at the youngest of students—those from kindergarten to grade 4. However, some of the units could be used as supplemental materials in the social studies curriculum of the fifth or sixth grade. These might include the chapters on heroes such as Elizabeth Cady Stanton, Dwight D. Eisenhower, and Henry Ford.

Some of the heroes we have chosen are among the most well known to children, e.g., George Washington, general and president. But others include the relatively obscure Snowflake Bentley, a Vermont farmer whose achievements spurred the development of photographic processes. In each case, we have chosen men and women who have possessed outstanding characteristics and achieved a high pinnacle of success in their chosen fields. All are worthy role models for youngsters and can be emulated in today's society, which often gives credence to violence and negative values.

The cast of heroes begins with the Virginia settlement of James Towne [*sic*] led by Captain John Smith and continues chronologically to a contemporary African American family celebrating the presence of their matriarchal grandmother on the Fourth of July. During this 400-year sweep of history, students will study real-life heroes such as Sacajawea, who led the Corps of Discovery across the Louisiana Purchase, and the prince of the piano, Duke Ellington, who wrote masterpieces for both jazz and classical tastes. There are fictional heroes who lived ordinary lives yet were heroic to their contemporaries, e.g., Lydia, the young gardener who raised the spirits of her family and friends during the days of the Great Depression, and Cecil, who coped with hardship and loss during the Civil War until he was finally reunited with those he loved.

We hope that the wide variety of subjects, which we have chosen, will give life to the definition, which we formulated. Hopefully other heroes will come to the forefront as topics of study because they are also exceptional people. But most of all, we hope that these units will help students become aware that perhaps it is also themselves and those around them who should strive to be the true heroes of our world.

Introduction

Each unit of this book begins with a summary of the story, related words used in the book, and related concepts or themes. This background material is followed by activities from each area of the curriculum—language arts, writing, social studies, math, science, the arts, the computer, and the library media center. There is also a puzzle and a list of references for each unit.

This book is subtitled *A Standards-Based Approach*. The writing of standards is an ongoing process that is taking place at both the state and national levels. With so many sets of standards available, it was impossible to use a specific set of standards that would assist everyone. Instead, we have studied many standards lists from various groups like the National Council of Teachers of English, the National Science Teachers Association, and the National Council of Teachers of Math. From these we made composite standards, which are given at the end of this introduction. They reflect the different facets of learning that children should master in the fields of math, English, social studies, science, and the arts. For example:

"Math-spatial" activities utilize visualization and spatial reasoning.

"English-genre" recommends reading a wide genre of literature.

"Social studies-maps" indicates the use of maps or geographical tools.

"Science-organisms" understands the interactions of organisms and their life cycles.

"Art-music connections" makes connections between music and other disciplines.

In making lesson plans, we do not recommend that the teacher use every activity. This would be far too overwhelming. Instead, the use of six or seven activities from different areas would produce an integrated unit. Or the emphasis could be on certain of the topic areas to coincide with the school curriculum—perhaps a science-math unit, or one that emphasizes a combination of social studies and the arts. The activities listed are the tools, which have been given to teachers to utilize as they meet the needs of their students.

The reference section of each unit is to be used by either teacher or student. For example, the teacher may know little or nothing of Alice Ramsey, who was the first woman to drive across the United States. There are Internet references to her life and her trip to fill this information gap. On the other hand, students may also read about Alice, but their focus of attention may be the photos of her and her automobile, a 1909 Maxwell touring car. In both cases, the articles offer additional information to complete a presentation.

We have suggested an outline of a unit that includes background information, activities from many different genres, and particular standards upon which to build units of instruction.

Although we have given specific activities to emulate, we hope these may intersect with tried-and-true activities teachers have used before, or they may be coupled with particular demands of the curriculum. The material is here! The heroes abound! Construct your own distinguished units of instruction. Above all, enjoy!

Standards and Abbreviations

MATHEMATICS

- Math-numbers: Understand numbers and use simple operations.

- Math-relations: Understand patterns and relationships.

- Math-spatial: Use visualization and spatial reasoning.

- Math-measurement: Understand and apply measurement.

- Math-questioning: Formulate questions, and collect and analyze data.

- Math-problem: Apply problem-solving strategies.

- Math-reasoning: Select and use reasoning methods.

- Math-communication: Express ideas precisely.

- Math-representations: Use various representations or communicate ideas.

ENGLISH/LANGUAGE ARTS

- English-genre: Read a wide range of literature: biography, history, and fiction.

- English-human experience: Understand many different dimensions of human experience.

- English-interpret: Draw upon many strategies to interpret text.

- English-audience: Use audience-appropriate language styles to communicate effectively.

- English-grammar: Apply knowledge of language structure, convention, spelling, and punctuation.

- English-research: Research issues and interests.

- English-sources: Use a variety of sources to obtain information, including computer networks and video, audio, and print media.

- English-diversity: Understand and respect the diversity of speaking and writing.

- English-native tongue: Use first-language skills to master English.

- English-cooperative learning: Participate in cooperative language learning.

- English-forms: Use language in various forms—written, spoken, and visual—for appropriate purposes.

SOCIAL STUDIES

- Social studies-maps: Use maps and other geographical tools.

- Social studies-place: Understand the physical and social human attributes of places.

- Social studies-migration: Understand the distribution and migration of people on the earth.

- Social studies-environment: Understand how people modify the environment.

- Social studies-resources: Understand that productive resources are limited.

- Social studies-distribution: Understand how goods and services are distributed.

- Social studies-economic incentives: Understand how people respond to economic incentives.

- Social studies-trade: Understand that people trade to obtain what they need.

- Social studies-competition: Understand how competition alters prices and supplies of goods and services.

- Social studies-government: Understand the role of government and the ways that laws can be made.

- Social studies-democracy: Understand the basic beliefs and principles of American democracy.

- Social studies-Constitution: Understand the basic role of the U.S. Constitution in American government.

- Social studies-nations: Understand how nations of the world interact.

- Social studies-rights: Understand the basic rights and responsibilities of American citizens.

- Social studies-community: Understand how the individual interacts within the family and community.

- Social studies-democratic values: Understand how the democratic values of the United States came to be.

- Social studies-world culture: Understand how the attributes of world cultures contribute to the United States.

- Social studies-inventors: Understand the major contributions of scientists and inventors, including their social and economic effects.

SCIENCE

- Science-inquiry: Develop skills to do scientific inquiry.

- Science-materials: Develop an understanding of materials and objects.

- Science-motion: Develop an understanding of motion of objects.

- Science-energy: Develop an understanding of light, heat, electricity, and magnetism.

- Science-organisms: Develop an understanding of organisms and their life cycles.

- Science-environments: Develop an understanding of the interaction of organisms and their environments.

- Science-earth materials: Develop an understanding of earth materials.

- Science-universe: Develop an understanding of the objects in the sky and their changes.

- Science-technology: Develop an understanding of the effects of science on technology.

- Science-health: Develop good personal health habits.

- Science-populations: Develop an understanding of changes in populations.

- Science-environmental change: Develop an understanding of changes in the environment.

- Science-natural resources: Develop an understanding of types of natural resources.

- Science-technology and society: Develop an understanding of the challenges between local values and technology.

ARTS

- Arts-voice: Develop the ability to sing on pitch and in rhythm alone and in groups.

- Arts-instruments: Develop the ability to perform music on simple instruments.

- Arts-improvise: Improvise simple melodies and rhythms.

- Arts-arrange: Arrange music to accompany text or pictures.

- Arts-notation: Read musical notation.

- Arts-musical forms: Listen to and understand various musical forms.

- Arts-musical connections: Make connections between music and other disciplines.

- Arts-music culture: Understand music in relation to history and culture.

- Arts-media: Understand and apply media, techniques, and processes.

- Arts-structures: Use knowledge of structures and functions.

- Arts-selection: Choose and evaluate a range of subject matter, symbols, and ideas.

- Arts-visual culture: Understand the visual arts in relation to history and cultures.

- Arts-appreciation: Reflect upon and assess the characteristics and merits of one's work and the work of others.

- Arts-visual connections: Make connections between visual arts and other disciplines.

CHAPTER 1

James Towne: Struggle for Survival

Written by Marcia Sewall
New York: Atheneum Books for Young Readers, 2001

SUMMARY

The journey to America took several months longer than anticipated. Stores were running low, and many passengers were unable to do the labor expected of them. Captain John Smith emerged as a leader of the struggling colony.

RELATED CONCEPTS

London Company	economics
venture	work
profit	starving time
colonization	

RELATED VOCABULARY

Orient	charter
territory	Roanoke
King's Council	peninsula
governor	settlement

ACTIVITIES

Language Arts

Working in small groups, have the students take one of the original entries written by members of the colony. "Translate" these passages into modern English. Another means of showing how our language is constantly changing is to look in a newer dictionary to see which words have been added to the language. Are there other words or phrases that you think should be in a future dictionary? (English-audience, English-research)

Many happenings kept the first settlers from leaving Bristol, England, according to schedule. Similarly, circumstances could keep a family from leaving for vacation. Label the following modern events according to this scale:

1—The incident is in need of great problem solving, and the trip may need to be postponed for several or more days.

2—The incident is quite serious and may take a day or two to resolve.

3—The incident is a minor inconvenience and can be cleared up in a matter of hours.

_____ Mom's purse has been misplaced.

_____ The wire on your sister's braces has broken.

_____ A driver has lost control of his car and smashed into your parked auto.

_____ The pet hamster is loose.

_____ There is a fire down the street in the next block.

_____ One of the front tires on the car is flat.

_____ Your former next-door neighbors drop by unexpectedly to visit.

_____ A dog breaks loose from its owner and bites your brother's leg.

_____ Your older brother takes a bad spill on his skateboard while waiting to leave.

_____ Dad forgot to cancel the newspaper during the trip.

Have students brainstorm answers to these problems. (Social studies-migration)

Which would be easier—a move from Bristol, England, to the Virginia colony in 1607 or a move between two states today? This would include arranging for children's education, finding health facilities, establishing a home, and so on. (Social studies-place)

Writing

Both Captain Christopher Newport and Captain John Smith led the colonists at different times. Both men were excellent leaders, yet it is Captain Smith who is usually remembered. Write why you think this is so. Which leader do you think was better? (English-research)

Social Studies

Locate the James River and Chesapeake Bay. This area is called the Tidewater. What other rivers empty into the bay? How were these waters helpful to the early settlers? (Social studies-maps, Social studies-place)

Science

One of the greatest problems for the colonists was the long amount of time between the planting of crops and the harvest. To replicate the sprouting process, put a wet sponge into a clear, plastic glass. Place several seeds such as beans or corn between the inside of the container and the sponge. Keep the sponge moist. Record the progress of the seeds in a plant journal. After the seeds sprout, what steps must be taken? (Science-organisms)

Mathematics

There are many mathematical facts given at the end of the book. Using this information, answer the following questions. (Math-relations)

1. The midsized ship was the _____.

2. The largest of the ships was the _____.

3. How many crew and passengers could be taken on all three ships at once? _____

4. Did the two smaller ships have tonnage capacity equal to the size of the *Susan Constant*? _____

5. If thirty-four passengers were sailing to Virginia, which ship would best fit their needs? _____

6. How many pounds is 120 tons? 40 tons? 20 tons? _____

Answers

1. The midsized ship was the *Godspeed*.

2. The largest of the ships was the *Susan Constant*.

3. How many crew and passengers could be taken on all three ships at once? 144.

4. Did the two smaller ships have tonnage capacity equal to the size of the *Susan Constant*? No.

5. If thirty-four passengers were sailing to Virginia, which ship would best fit their needs? the *Godspeed*.

6. How many pounds is 120 tons? 240,000 lbs. 40 tons? 80,000 lbs. 20 tons? 40,000 lbs.

Have the students use this information to make additional problems for each other.

Measure out the size of the *Susan Constant* on the playground. Put fifty-four students (passengers) inside this replica. Would they have had much room for themselves and their belongings?

The Arts

The James Towne colony was begun at the same time that playwright William Shakespeare was writing in England. Look through books about sixteenth- and seventeenth-century theater to see the manner of clothing that the people wore. Using these examples, design other clothing in this style. (Arts-visual, Arts-culture)

Computer

Watersheds must be preserved and protected. What is a watershed? Use the Internet to define this word and find justification for this statement. (Social studies-environment, Science-environment)

Library Media Center

Find references to Pocahontas in various library books. Compare these articles with the version of her life as portrayed in the Walt Disney movie. (Arts-media, Arts-visual connections)

Puzzle

The following words are found in the crossword puzzle:

Susan Constant	James
governor	mosquitoes
Godspeed	starving time
Chesapeake Bay	Newport
Pocahontas	Orient

REFERENCES

www.apva.org/history/jsmith.html. A portrait of Smith accompanies this biographical sketch of Smith.

www.apva.org/history/pocahont.html. Much biographical information accompanies this Pocahontas portrait, along with further references to her life.

www.jamestown.org. This site contains the mission statement for the Jamestown Society as well as information about Jamestown itself, Captain Smith, Pocahontas, and other related people and terms.

www.libraryreference.org/roanoke.html. Little is known of the fate of the Roanoke Island colonists.

Across

3. Insects that were a great nuisance to the colonists.

5. The person in change of the government.

7. An Indian girl.

8. A time of great food shortage.

9. The colonist hoped to find a water route to this area.

10. The colony was named for this king.

Down

1. A governor before John Smith.

2. The largest of the ships that brought settlers.

4. The rivers flowed into this body of water.

6. The second largest of the ships from England.

Answer to puzzle appears on page 125.

CHAPTER **2**

Sleds on Boston Common

Written by Louise Borden

New York: Margaret McElderry Books, 2000

SUMMARY

When Henry Price and his classmates decided to go sledding during their lunch break from school, they had no idea they would meet General Thomas Gage. However, the general listened to Henry's appeal and agreed to let the children slide on the Commons, where the British troops were quartered.

RELATED CONCEPTS

courage

freedom

rights of citizens

RELATED VOCABULARY

common	port
harbor	"Lobster backs"
punish	barracks
patriots	bayonet

ACTIVITIES

Language Arts

The Intolerable Acts closed the Port of Boston to trade. Other Intolerable Acts included the following:

A demand that colonists provide barracks and supplies to the British troops

A limit to the power of the Massachusetts government (English-interpret, Social studies-government, Social studies-trade)

What does "intolerable" mean? Discuss why these acts were so unbearable to the colonists. Are there things that would be intolerable to the students—e.g., a broken Play Station? A best friend moving? And so forth. (English-human experience, English-cooperative learning)

Henry was very brave to talk to General Gage. Was there a time when the students needed to talk to a person in authority—e.g., the principal or a policeman? Role-play situations where the children ask for assistance from an older person—e.g., asking for longer recess time, handing in a project late, or organizing a school trip? (English-audience, English-cooperative learning)

After discussing the roles of Britain and the colonists during the 1770s, organize a debate. Students who believe the British had a right to impose the Intolerable Acts will oppose those who believe the colonists were justified in defying the acts. Allow planning time for students to write statements supporting their points of view. (English-audience, Social studies-government)

Writing

Write a journal page similar to one Henry might write. How did you feel when you saw the soldiers? Did General Gage scare you? Were you pleased when you were able to go sliding again? (English-grammar, Social studies-community)

From the information given in this book, predict what will happen in the colonies in 1775. (Social studies-democratic values, English-interpretation)

Social Studies

On a map of the United States, locate the city of Boston. Why did this city become an important seaport? (Social studies-place, English-research)

On a street map of Boston, you will find many historical places. Locate the Paul Revere House, the Old North Church, Faneuil Hall, the South Meeting House, the Soldiers Monument, and the Freedom Trail. Locate Long Wharf, where the men went to search for work, and the Common, where the story takes place. (Social studies-maps, Social studies-distribution)

Science

This story takes place in the winter. How much snow does Boston accumulate each winter? Compare this to the snowfall where the students live or to other cities that the students know. (Science-inquiry, Science-earth, Science-materials)

Mathematics

There was one British soldier for every five colonists in Boston. That means about 3,000 soldiers. How many colonists lived in Boston? Why did Britain keep so many soldiers quartered there? What was the effect on the colonists? (Math-numbers, Math-reasoning)

Boston had 15,000 citizens in 1774. How many people live in Boston today? How does this compare to the community where the students live? (Math-questioning)

The Arts

Have students design posters showing their point of view. Colonists may wish to use phrases such as "Down with the British," "No more Lobster backs," and "British go home." The Loyalist colonials might say, "God save the king," "Britain rules the seas," and "loyalty to England." (Arts-media)

The colonial soldiers sang while they marched. One of their favorite songs that they sang was "Yankee Doodle." (Arts-music connections, Social studies-world culture)

Chorus

Yankee Doodle keep it up, Yankee Doodle Dandy
Mind the music and the step, and with the girls be handy.

Verse

Fath'r and I went down to camp, along with Captain Good'in,
And there we saw the men and boys, as thick as hasty pudding.

Repeat Chorus

Verse

And there was Captain Washington, upon a slapping stallion,
A giving orders to his men, I guess there was a million.

Repeat Chorus

Computer

There is much information on the Internet relating to this book. Use the key words "Intolerable Acts" and "American Revolution" to locate Web sites. (English-sources)

Library Media Center

Using information found in the Library Media Center, make a bulletin board display of events leading up to the American Revolution. Begin with the Intolerable Acts. (Social studies-democracy)

Puzzle

Using words from the story, complete the following cloze procedure. (English-Interpret)

Henry was very excited! Today was his _____ and for a present his father had given him a _____. All morning in school, Henry was very _____. When the lunch break arrived, the boys ran to _____ _____. They found hundreds of troops standing on the boys' _____. Henry summoned up his courage and spoke to _____ _____, the commander-in-chief. The general agreed that the boys should be _____ to sled on Boston Common. Henry remembered the general's act of kindness long after the general sailed for _____.

Possible answers: birthday, sled, excited or happy, Boston Common, sliding spot or favorite hill, General Gage, allowed or able, England or Britain

Answer to Puzzle

Henry was very excited! Today was his <u>birthday</u> and for a present his father had given him a <u>sled</u>. All morning in school, Henry was very <u>excited/happy</u>. When the lunch break arrived, the boys ran to <u>Boston</u> <u>Common</u>. They found hundreds of troops standing on the boys' <u>sliding spot/favorite hill</u>. Henry summoned up his courage and spoke to <u>General Gage</u>, the commander-in-chief. The general agreed that the boys should be <u>allowed/able</u> to sled on Boston Common. Henry remembered the general's act of kindness long after the general sailed for <u>England/Britain.</u>

REFERENCES

Forbes, Esther. *Johnny Tremain*. New York: Yearling Books, 1987. A young boy in prewar Boston gets involved with the events of the day.

Kirkpatrick, Katherine. *Red Coats and Petticoats*. New York: Holiday House, 1999. This is a story of secrets and spies during the Revolution.

www.historyplace.com/unitedstates/revolution/teaparty. Facts about the Boston Tea Party are outlined.

www.kidsport.com/RefLib/USA/History/AmericanRevolution/IntolerableActs.htm. This special version of prerevolutionary events is especially for youngsters.

www.ushistory.org/declaration/related/intolerable.htm. This Web site gives details of the Intolerable Acts.

CHAPTER 3

George Washington's Teeth

Written by Deborah Chandra and Madeleine Comora

New York: Farrar, Straus and Giroux, 2003

SUMMARY

George Washington was plagued throughout his career by poor dental health. But through his persistence, he coped with the problem and became a military and political giant.

RELATED CONCEPTS

redcoats

Revolutionary War

tooth disease

dental care

RELATED VOCABULARY

invaded	molar
attack	cuspid
fort	bicuspid
cannons	false teeth

ACTIVITIES

Language Arts

Heroes are often regarded as "larger than life." However, this book doesn't show Washington in this light. Instead, he is portrayed as someone with personal problems who also became famous. Discuss the different facets of this leader. Why is he remembered as a great person? (Social studies-democratic values, Social studies-government)

What other persons—historical or modern—are considered to be "larger than life"? What contemporary persons might this include? (English-interpret)

Writing

In 1777–1778, Washington's army wintered over at Valley Forge, Pennsylvania. Supplies were nearly nonexistent, and there was much suffering among the men. Compose a letter that might be written by one of Washington's men to a loved one. (English-grammar)

Washington was constantly writing to the Continental Congress, which governed the colonies. His requests were for supplies and money. Write a letter from Washington emphasizing the reasons for these requests. (English-grammar)

Social Studies

Locate these places mentioned in the book—New York City, the Delaware River, Valley Forge, and Mount Vernon. Other important battles that led to colonial freedom were Saratoga, the turning point of the war, and Yorktown, the final battle. Where are they located? (Social studies-place)

Science

Dentistry has made monumental strides since the days of Washington. Have someone in this field speak to the class or gather some folders on tooth replacement, cosmetic dentistry, and other dentistry topics. This would also include the use of braces, dentures, bridges, and implants. (Science-technology)

Mathematics

Human teeth are described in the following charts:

Baby teeth—each jaw has:

four incisors

two cuspids

four molars

Permanent teeth—each jaw has:

four incisors

two cuspids

four bicuspids

six molars

Make a bar graph comparing the baby teeth of a person to his or her permanent teeth. (Science-organisms, Math-spatial)

The Arts

The minuet was a very popular dance in Washington's day. Listen to minuets written by these popular composers: Telemann, Rameau, Handel, Scarlatti, Bach, Haydn, and Mozart. Compare these to modern dance music. (Arts-musical forms)

Computer

Use the computer to locate national battlefields, national parks, or monuments that are memorials to action during the Revolutionary War. In what states are these memorials found? Do these coincide with the locations of major battles? (Social studies-maps)

Library Media Center

Portraits of Washington usually show him as a somber person. Check the portraits shown in library sources. Are they similar in appearance? Why would this be so? (Arts-visual culture)

Puzzle

The following words are used in the crossword puzzle:

dentist	Valley Forge
teeth	Mount Vernon
Delaware	Potomac
Martha	false teeth
president	portrait

REFERENCES

Adler, David A. *A Picture Book of George Washington*. New York: Holiday House, 1990. This is one in a series of books about great Americans.

Small, David. *George Washington's Cows*. New York: Farrar, Straus and Giroux, 1994. This book humorously gives the "real" reason why George Washington entered politics.

www.nps.gov/gewa/. Educational programs by grade level are part of this Web site on Washington's birthplace.

www.Whitehouse.gov/history/presidents/gw1.html. Information about the presidents can be found using this Web site.

George Washington's Teeth

Across

1. River that passes Mount Vernon and Washington, DC

4. George Washington depended on these to chew his food.

6. Highest political office in the United States.

7. George Washington's wife.

8. Washington crossed this river.

9. A doctor who works on teeth.

Down

2. George Washington's home in Virginia.

3. A place in Pennsylvania where the Continental Army experienced a bad winter.

5. Parts of the body that we use to chew food.

6. Picture of a person made by a painter.

Answer to puzzle appears on page 125.

CHAPTER 4

How We Crossed the West:
The Adventures of Lewis and Clark

Written by Rosalyn Schanzer

Washington, DC: National Geographic Society, 1997

SUMMARY

Lewis and Clark and their Corps of Discovery were the first persons to explore the Louisiana Purchase and the land to the Pacific Ocean. Their science and geographical insights and their contacts with various Indian tribes were invaluable sources of knowledge.

RELATED CONCEPTS

Louisiana Purchase

transcontinental

Manifest Destiny

Corps of Discovery

RELATED VOCABULARY

keelboat	warriors
pirogues	Mandan
rudder	Shoshoni
recruits	Nez Perce
Seamus	pipe of peace
York	scalps
buffalo	interpreter
prairie dogs	Cascade Mountains
antelope	Missouri River

ACTIVITIES

Language Arts

To introduce the trip, ask all students to stand up as the teacher describes the beginning of the journey of Lewis and Clark. As each student finds an aspect of the trip that he or she could not tolerate, have him or her sit down. Are there any students left who would want to go on the trip? Conditions to consider are no motorized vehicles, no refrigeration, no flashlights, no telephones, and no maps. (English-human experience)

Make a list of ten important items that you would need on an exploratory trip in 1803. These would be carried on a keelboat, along with members of the party. If you were going to follow the same route today, what would be the ten most essential items for a modern journey? (English-resources)

Writing

Write a journal page from the viewpoint of various members of the party—Lewis, Clark, Sacajewea, York the slave, the Indians who befriended them, or others. (English-grammar)

Social Studies

On a large map, locate the Louisiana Purchase as well as the routes taken by the explorers to the Pacific Ocean and on their return trip. What future U.S. states would be carved out of this territory? Did Lewis and Clark go beyond the boundaries of the purchase? (Social studies-maps)

President Thomas Jefferson asked Lewis and Clark to undertake this expedition. What else is known about this president of the United States? Where would you go to visit his home and library? (Science-natural resources, Social studies-place)

Science

Lewis and Clark studied and sketched the flora and fauna that they saw on their journey. Have the students sketch the plants and animals that are native to their area. Use these as part of a bulletin board display. (Science-organisms, Arts-media)

Mathematics

Calculate the distance from Pittsburgh to the Pacific Ocean and back. Remember that the two leaders chose different routes on the way back. (Math-relations, Math-measurement)

The Arts

Make sketches of Native Americans who befriended the group, especially the Nez Perce, the Shoshoni, and the Mandan. Add these settlements to the map of the Louisiana Territory along with any other drawings of the trip. (Arts-media)

Computer

Use the Internet or other sources to learn more about Sacajawea. Some say she died at twenty-five. Others claim she lived into her eighties. Compare these two different scenarios. (Social studies-world culture)

Library Media Center

The bicentennial of the Lewis and Clark expedition saw the publication of myriad books about this trip. Have the media specialist share some of these books from the school library. (English-cooperative learning)

Puzzle

The following words are used in the crossword puzzle:

Louisiana	Shoshoni
France	York
Sacajewea	Mandan
Missouri	Rockies
Pacific	Jefferson
Seamus	

REFERENCES

www.jum.edu/madison/lewispurchase.htm. This site contains a color map of the Louisiana Purchase.

www.lewis-clark.org. This is an in-depth look at the Lewis and Clark expedition.

www.monticello.org/education/resources/books.html. This is an excellent source of information about the expedition.

www.nps.gov/led/. The National Trail and the Junior Web Ranger program are highlighted in this site.

How We Crossed the West: The Adventures of Lewis and Clark

Across

3. The tribe that sheltered the Corps of Discovery during the winter.

5. Sacajewea's tribe.

7. The mountains crossed by the Corps of Discovery.

9. It was purchased from France.

10. The dog that went with the Corps of Discovery.

11. Country that owned much of the southern and midwestern United States.

Down

1. Western end of the journey.

2. The river traveled by the Corps of Discovery.

4. The slave member of the Corps of Discovery.

6. President of the United States who sent the Corps of Discovery.

8. An Indian guide.

Answer to puzzle appears on page 126.

CHAPTER 5

New York's Bravest

Written by Mary Pope Osborne
New York: Alfred A. Knopf, 2002

SUMMARY

The life of a firefighter at the time of this book is different from how it is today. Still, there will always be heroes to admire.

RELATED CONCEPTS

burning

rescuing

bravery

RELATED VOCABULARY

oxygen	alarm
flame	extinguisher
smoke	prevention
temperature	chief
fire truck	firefighter

ACTIVITIES

Language Arts

Firefighters have much to teach us about fires. Arrange for a firefighter to give an assembly program. Have additional small-group sessions for in-depth coverage.
Questions to be asked include the following:

How are firefighters trained?

How can fires be prevented?

What should students do if there is a fire at home or at school? (English-sources, Science-technology)

Writing

Write an alternate ending for this story. Begin at the point that Mose does not come out of the burning building. (English-grammar)

Social Studies

Visit a fire station and become familiar with their equipment. How fast can the firefighters be ready and on their way to a fire? Who will be involved? What assignments must be addressed? How is the location of the fire known? (Social studies-place)

Science

Fires occur when an object is heated and reacts with oxygen. This reaction raises the temperature around the object, and it begins to glow or burn. To put out a fire, some of the oxygen must be removed or the temperature must be reduced. How does the firefighter accomplish this? How can fires be extinguished at home? (Science-energy)

Mathematics

Many fire departments are facing great budget cuts. Others are getting along on less. How are these example fire departments faring? (Math-relations)

The budget for the Westmont Fire Department was $239,714 last year. This year, it has been cut to $194,835.00. How much money was cut from the budget?

The present budget for the Acadia Fire Department was $400,098. If there is a 25 percent increase in their budget this year, will they be able to buy a new fire truck that costs $75,000?

Briarwood Acres spends 60 percent of its budget on personnel and 40 percent on equipment. If they cut 10 percent of the equipment allotment, how much will they cut out of a $1,480,234 budget?

The Arts

Design a poster for Fire Prevention Week using the knowledge learned from the firefighter's visit. (Arts-media)

Computer

Using the key words "history of fire trucks," find Internet entries about vintage and modern fire trucks. (Science-technology, Science-technology and society)

Also locate the Web site for the International Association of Fire Fighters. What is their purpose? Does your local fire department belong to this group? (Social studies-economics)

Library Media Center

Many books on firefighters have been written for very young children. Have students read these books to children in kindergarten or the first grade. What questions do they have? (English-research)

Puzzle

The following words are scrambled:

oxygen	smoke
firefighter	equipment
truck	hose
alarm	ladder
extinguisher	engine
chief	water

These are the scrambled words:

goxney	darled
kmseo	gneeni
hecfi	maral
hifgretfier	rewta
ktcur	temnpiueq
sohe	

REFERENCES

Yee, Wong Herbert. *Fireman Small.* Boston: Houghton Mifflin, 1998. This and the following book are for younger readers.

Yee, Wong Herbert. *Fireman Small to the Rescue.* Boston: Houghton Mifflin, 2002.

www.fdny.net/. The work of many firefighters is given in the pages of this free quarterly magazine, e.g., children who lost someone close in the 9/11 disaster are eligible to attend camp for free.

www.sparky.org/. The whole family will enjoy Sparky and his friends.

CHAPTER 6

Henry Hikes to Fitchburg

Written by D. B. Johnson
Boston: Houghton Mifflin, 2000

SUMMARY

Philosopher Henry David Thoreau and a friend vie to see who can make the journey from Concord to Fitchburg in the least amount of time. Henry spends his time on the journey doing odd jobs and enjoying nature.

RELATED CONCEPTS

speed

competition

back-to-nature

industrialism

energy

RELATED VOCABULARY

hike	press
work	courthouse
wood box	grazing
walking stick	raft
ferns	mill

ACTIVITIES

Language Arts

Henry David Thoreau wanted to protect and preserve nature. Select several passages from his *Walden Pond* or use excerpts from the Internet. How do these enhance and explain the text of the picture book about Thoreau? (English-genre)

One of Thoreau's most famous quotes is that some individuals "march to a different drummer." Exactly what does this mean? Do any students feel that they are the kind of person that Thoreau describes? (English-interpret)

Everything that Thoreau did on the way to Fitchburg was enjoyable to him. However, students may wish to categorize Thoreau's actions as "work activities" or "fun activities." Is the choice easily made? What do the students consider to be "work" or "fun"? Do circumstances affect their choices—e.g., having to babysit for free, or babysitting for money? (Social studies-economic incentives)

Some people think of Thoreau as a "hermit" or "recluse." In his works, Thoreau mentions that he often walked into town and regularly entertained visitors in his home. Does this support the idea that he was reclusive? (English-interpret)

Writing

Thoreau did live a more solitary life than most persons of his time. Have the students decide if they would prefer this solitary life to their life today. They should justify their reasoning process. (English-grammar, English-human experience)

Explain that Thoreau and his friend are going to Fitchburg—one by walking and the other by train. Just before the end of the book, have the students select which man they think will win and why. (Math-relations, Social studies-maps)

Social Studies

On a map of Massachusetts, locate Concord and Fitchburg. What roads would a driver use to make the journey today? If map-reading software is available, zero in on the geography of these two towns and trace any alternate paths. (Social studies-maps)

Science

Thoreau pressed flowers in the pages of his large book. This can be done with flowers the students gather using a book or using a professional-quality plant press available at scientific equipment stores. For best results, choose flowers that will lie fairly flat. The flowers should remain undisturbed for two weeks. Flowers can be sealed in pieces of clear contact paper to make bookmarks, dream catchers, room decorations, and other items. (Science-organisms)

Mathematics

The companion book to this one is *Henry Builds a Cabin*. In the "Economy" section of *Walden Pond*, Thoreau itemizes how much he spends for materials to build the cabin. Compare these numbers to prices in a home builder's newspaper ad. (Math-relations, Math-problems)

The Arts

Pastoral music is that which is written in response to nature or a country setting. Ask the music teacher to recommend some pieces that would be pastoral in nature and would complement

Thoreau's way of life. How do the students feel upon listening to this genre of music? (Arts-music connections)

Computer

Thoreau is considered to be one of the first environmentalists in this country. On the Internet, find a definition of this word as well as the basic goals of these people. For example, Theodore Roosevelt was called an environmentalist because he believed in preserving much of nature. Groups such as the Sierra Club and the Nature Conservancy are considered to have environmentalism in their agenda. (Science-environments)

Library Media Center

In an atlas of the United States, look up Massachusetts—one of the original thirteen colonies. What historical and present-day knowledge do you find in this entry? Which large city is closest to Concord and Fitchburg? (Social studies-maps, Social studies-place, Social studies-resources)

Puzzle

The following words from the story are scrambled:

stream	weed
stones	trees
swamp	river
pond	blackberries
flower	fields

These are the scrambled words:

dopn	lerowf
silfed	pawsm
maetrs	sesotn
stree	klarriebesbc
eewd	revir

REFERENCES

Johnson, D. B. *Henry Builds a Cabin*. Boston: Houghton Mifflin, 2002. This is the companion book to *Henry Hikes to Fitchburg* and describes how Thoreau built his home and entertained friends.

Thoreau, Henry David. *Walden: A Fully Annotated Edition*. New Haven, CT: Yale University Press, 2004. Thoreau was a prolific writer who left many essays for his readers.

www.nanosft.com/walden/essays/index.html. Many of Thoreau's writings are included on this site, including "Economy," about house building.

www.nanosft.com/walden/october/index.html. Photos taken in and around Walden Pond in October 1998 show a pastoral setting.

CHAPTER 7

Cecil's Story

Written by George Ella Lyon
New York: Orchard Books, 1991

SUMMARY

When Mother leaves to tend Father after he is wounded in the Civil War, Cecil speculates on what life will be like when Father returns home. Many changes will need to be made to accommodate his dad's handicap, e.g., Cecil's role in running the farm will be expanded.

RELATED CONCEPTS

war

bravery

RELATED VOCABULARY

journey

mules

harvest

amputate

ACTIVITIES

Language Arts

Modern wars can be seen live and on the spot because of today's technology. Reporters can cover every aspect of the fighting as well as activities away from the front. In the nineteenth century, however, it was often days before citizens had any news of fighting. Even with the use of the telegraph, newspapers could not receive information as quickly as people wanted. Is it necessary, today, for reporters to provide on-the-spot war coverage in all its detail? What purpose does this entail? (Social studies-place, English-interpret)

After the long separation, how would the father and son react? Would they be nervous, anxious, sad, scared, or happy? Write a description of their meeting, or choose a few lines of dialog. (English-human experience, English-grammar)

Assign topics for short research papers. Suggestions include the following. (English-research)

uniforms	the field doctor
weapons	maps
music	state regiments
transportation	individual battles
flags	biographies
ships	

Writing

Write a letter from the point of view of Cecil, the mother, or the father. What is their involvement in the war effort? How would they feel about the war? (English-grammar, English-human experience)

Social Studies

Make a time line of the major events of the Civil War from its beginning at Fort Sumter in 1861 until the Appomattox surrender in 1865. (Social studies-government)

On a large map of the eastern United States, indicate the northern states and the southern states. Place the capitals of Washington, DC, and Richmond, Virginia, in their places. Add markers for major battles. (Social studies-maps)

Using a world almanac, look up the national battlefields that are Civil War battle sites. They are listed as national battlefields, national battlefield parks, and national military parks. Locate these sites on a Civil War–era map. If there is a battlefield nearby, visit it and find its significance. Another alternative is to assign each student a battle to research. (Social studies-maps, English-research)

Science

Medical practice in battlefield hospitals was unbelievably crude compared to modern practices. More men died of disease and infection than from war injuries. Research the equipment and procedures that these doctors had at their disposal and how they carried out their jobs—e.g., was any anesthesia available? Were sanitary procedures carried out in the field hospitals? (Science-technology)

Mathematics

The armies were divided into units consisting of a certain number of men:

Squad	10 men
Platoon	20 men
Company	100 men
Regiment	1,000 men
Brigade	3,000 men
Division	9,000 men
Corps	27,000 men

Using these numbers, make up math problems—e.g., how many platoons make up a company? How many divisions equal a corps? And what do two companies and a regiment equal? (Math-relations, Math-questioning)

The Arts

Design regimental flags that could have been used in the Civil War. The information on these flags might include a regimental number, a state's name, and the nicknames and ethnic background of the soldiers. (Arts-media)

Computer

Two ironclad ships staged a historical battle during the war. Find information on the *Merrimack* and the *Monitor*. (Science-technology)

Library Media Center

Read other books about the Civil War, including *The Blue and the Gray* by Eve Bunting. (English-human experience)

Puzzle

The following words are used in the crossword puzzle.

amputee	hardship
brave	neighbors
Civil War	plow
farm	soil
fishing	harvest

Across

3. A time when necessities are scarce.

7. Cared for Cecil while his family was away.

8. A person who has lost a limb.

Down

1. A place where crops are grown.

2. A pastime enjoyed by Cecil and his father.

3. To bring in the crops.

4. The layer of earth in which plants grow.

5. A conflict between northern and southern states.

6. To be courageous.

9. To prepare the ground for planting.

Answer to puzzle appears on page 126.

REFERENCES

Bunting, Eve. *The Blue and the Gray*. New York: Scholastic, 2001. As new homes are being built, two young boys try to visualize when the land was a Civil War battlefield.

www.americancivilwar.com/. Information can be accessed using key words, battles, dates, or persons.

www.civilwar.com/. Each choice links the reader to a different aspect of the war; some photos are included.

CHAPTER 8

Going West

Written by Jean Van Leeuwen
New York: Dial Books for Young Children, 1992

SUMMARY

A family of five endures the hardships of a wagon journey to reach a new home in the midwestern United States. Despite Mama's loneliness and the hard work that they face, the family knows it was a wise choice.

RELATED CONCEPTS

pioneering

westward movement

barter economy

RELATED VOCABULARY

wagon	spinning wheel
canvas	quilts
prairie	bucket
mounds	stable

ACTIVITIES

Language Arts

Discuss moving. How was this done in pioneer days? How is it done today? Ask someone from a local moving and storage company to speak to the class. Ask questions about how to pack, the size of moving vans, and how long it takes a moving van to reach its destination. What if something is damaged during the move? (Social studies-migration)

What would be the most valuable belonging for the students to pack if they were to move? Would they keep it with them or have it go on the moving van? (Social studies-rcsources)

Writing

Make a Venn diagram comparing life on the prairie with life today. Investigate topics such as education, chores, entertainment, transportation, clothing, and food. Add other topics that interest the students. (English-interpret, Math-spatial)

Pioneers faced many hardships on the journey—e.g., inclement weather, sickness, and loneliness. Write a page from a journal describing at least two of these or other hardships. (English-grammar, English-human experience)

Social Studies

Hundreds of thousands of pioneers moved to the Great Plains area of the United States. Locate these states on a map of the United States—North Dakota, South Dakota, Nebraska, Iowa, Kansas, and Minnesota. (Social studies-maps)

Science

Mama said that she wanted a tree. She probably hoped that the tree would provide shade. What kind of tree should she get? Look in a book that describes different types of trees—fruit trees, shade trees, ornamental trees, and evergreen trees. Also check the growth rates of the various trees. (Science-environments)

Mathematics

The cargo section of a Conestoga wagon was ten feet by four feet. Into this space the family put food, clothing, photos, books, toys, cooking utensils, farm tools, and nails. The family also sought cover in the wagon when the weather was inclement. Mark off a 10×4-foot space in the classroom. Label boxes with the names of the items most commonly carried. Fit these boxes into the forty square feet to see how crowded life became on the journey. (Math-spatial, Math-measurement)

Papa often "bartered" for the goods that the family needed. What does this term mean? What areas of the world still have a "barter economy"? (Social studies-trade)

Papa could average ten miles a day when he walked to town. How far could he go in three days, in seven days, and so on? If he walked for one and a half days, how far did he go? If he took the ox, could he go faster? Have the students make up other problems using these figures. (Math-reasoning)

A wagon train also averaged ten miles a day. How far would they go in a week? In a month? How long would it take to go 2,300 miles? (Math-reasoning)

The Arts

Make a floor plan for a 12×12-foot cabin. All of the items from the Conestoga wagon need a place to be stored, plus there must be room for the family. How could this be accomplished? (Arts-media, Math-spatial)

Computer

Assign students a research topic in which they study one of the Plains states. Use information from the Internet, atlases, or informational books for the report. (English-research, Social studies-place)

Library Media Center

The media center should have several books about the United States to assist students with research on their state. (English-research, Social studies-place)

Puzzle

Each number in the statement has a corresponding letter. When the letters have all been filled in, you will have an important line from the story.

a	b	c	d	e	f	g	h	i	j	k	l	m	n	o	p	q	r	s
1	2	3	4	5	6	7	8	9	10	11	12	13	14	15	16	17	18	19

t	u	v	w	x	y	z
20	21	22	23	24	25	26

Mother's lament about their new home:

15 8   13 25!   20 8 9 19   9 19   1   12 15 14 5 19 15 13 5   12 1 14 4.

Answer to the puzzle:

Oh my! This is a lonesome land.

REFERENCES

Bunting, Eve. *Dandelions*. San Diego, CA: Voyager Books, 1995. *Dandelions* is very similar in content to *Going West*. The two could be compared and contrasted.

Wilder, Laura Ingalls. *Little House on the Prairie*. New York: HarperCollins, 1953. This is the second volume in the Little House series.

http://oregontrail.blm.gov/Index.htm. The Oregon Trail Interpretive Center answers many queries about life on the way west.

www.endofthetrail.org/histhome.html. Sections on all areas of interest, including the role of women and blacks on the trail.

CHAPTER 9

The Ballot Box Battle

Written by Emily Arnold McCully
New York: Alfred A. Knopf, Dragonfly Books, 1996

SUMMARY

Elizabeth Cady Stanton tells her young female neighbor of the fight for women's right to vote. Mrs. Stanton also encourages her to learn to do things that young women are not expected to do in the nineteenth century, e.g., horseback jumping.

RELATED CONCEPTS

discrimination

franchise

RELATED VOCABULARY

suffragette	resolution
vote	poll
Election Day	ballot box

ACTIVITIES

Language Arts

Read and analyze the 14th Amendment, which freed the slaves; the 15th Amendment, which stated that there should be no discrimination because of race, color, or condition of servitude; and the 19th Amendment, which gave women the right to vote. These amendments are all part of the U.S. Constitution. Why was it necessary to make constitutional amendments to grant these rights? Would a simple state law have sufficed? (Social studies-rights, Social studies-Constitution)

Many women fought for women's rights, including Susan B. Anthony, Elizabeth Cady Stanton, Lucretia Mott, Carrie Nation, Amelia Bloomer, and Alice Paul. These women's lives can be researched by small groups of students. How are they remembered today (e.g., the Alice Paul House is a refuge from domestic violence)? (Social studies-rights)

Writing

Write a speech to be given at a "Right to Vote" rally. Or give a biographical introduction for someone who will speak at the rally. (English-grammar, English-audience)

Social Studies

Locate the National Women's Rights Historical Park in Seneca Falls, New York. What is the purpose of this park? What can be learned about the fight for women's rights? (Social studies-place, Social studies-maps)

Science

This book takes place at a time when there were none of the modern conveniences that we take for granted—e.g., electricity, cars, and computers. Discuss how people would have been able to put their causes before the public and how they would influence people and win converts. How were women's rights presented to the public? How were campaigns for elected officials conducted? (Science-technology)

Mathematics

Does it matter if women vote in an election? In Mrs. Jones's class, there are 16 students—8 boys and 8 girls. In a class election, the winner must get at least 9 votes. Will the candidate win if 6 boys and 2 girls support the candidate? Will the candidate win if 5 boys and 3 girls support the candidate?

If all the boys vote for the candidate, how many girls must vote for the candidate? Make up further examples. (Math-reasoning)

The Arts

Suffragettes held many rallies as they fought for certain rights, such as the right to vote. Design a poster that would attract attention and motivate persons to attend the rally. (Arts-media)

Computer

Is it possible to register to vote in your community by using the Internet? How many registered voters are listed in your area? Are they Republicans, Democrats, or Independents? How many voters turned out in the last election? What is this percentage? How could students help increase the number of those who vote? (Social studies-government)

Library Media Center

Using a world almanac or other resource book, find the names of women who were "first" in their field—e.g., the first woman Supreme Court justice, first woman to pilot the Atlantic, first woman astronaut, and first woman governor. (English-research)

Puzzle

The following words are used in the crossword puzzle:

vote	ballot
amendment	discrimination
suffrage	candidate
revolution	equal education
Stanton	

REFERENCES

www.betterworldlinks.org/book41zh.htm. Myriad references are given for American and English suffragettes who fought for women's right to vote.

www.mith2.umd.edu/WomensStudies/ReadingRoom/History/Vote/75-suffragists.html.

http://pbskids.org/stantonanthony/. Especially for kids, this is the story of Susan B. Anthony and Elizabeth Cady Stanton.

www.suffragist.com/timeline.htm.

www.susanbanthonyhouse.org/. The Susan B. Anthony house and its memorabilia pay honor to this great leader. The home can be visited in Seneca Falls, NY.

The Ballot Box Battle

Across

2. Both men and women have the same chance to learn.

4. The right to vote.

6. One who runs for public office.

7. A complete change from the way things were done.

8. Women wished to have a right to . . .

9. A suffragette.

Down

1. Withholding of rights because of gender or race.

3. An addition or change made to a public document.

5. A paper on which political candidates are listed.

Answer to puzzle appears on page 126.

CHAPTER 10

Clara Barton

Written by Candice Ransom
New York: Backpack Books, 2003

SUMMARY

After many years of being a schoolteacher, Clara devoted her energy to caring for and re-locating injured soldiers from the American Civil War. In her later years, she founded the American Red Cross to aid victims of war and natural disaster.

RELATED CONCEPTS

suffragette   women in society

abolitionist   emergency aid

Angel of the Battlefield   internationalism

slavery

RELATED VOCABULARY

tomboy   warehouse

volunteer   disaster

battlefield   smallpox

bandage

ACTIVITIES

Language Arts

Use a graphic organizer to write down the facts of Clara Barton's life. You might try this form. (English-interpret)

Person studied

Setting

Time

Characters

Problem

   Event

   Event

   Event (and so on)

Outcome

Have a person who is very knowledgeable about Clara Barton produce a one-woman show of her life. The actress would be dressed in a costume for the period. She would take questions about her life, her work during the Civil War, and the founding of the American Red Cross. Questions should be submitted before the interview to allow for appropriate responses. (English-audience)

For over a century, the American Red Cross has assisted individuals and families when a disaster strikes. These bad times include tornados, hurricanes, floods, forest fires, hazardous waste spills, train derailments, terrorist attacks, and wars. Have someone from the local Red Cross chapter speak about the work of this organization during local tragedies. How do Red Cross chapters help in instances where the devastation is widespread? (Social studies-resources, Social studies-environments)

Writing

Clara had no governmental support for her work with Civil War victims. In a letter from Clara to President Lincoln, state her case for needing government funds. Describe the conditions on the battlefields and in the field hospitals, and what could be accomplished with funding. (English-grammar, English-human experience)

The American Red Cross must raise its own funding. Write a flyer asking for money. This could be sent to the citizens of the local community. Be sure to include examples of work that the Red Cross has done in the community, and express the need to raise funds. (English-audience, English-visual connections)

Social Studies

Locate the Clara Barton National Historical Site in Glen Echo, Maryland. What attractions can be seen there? How far away from the site are the students? Is a trip to Glen Echo possible? (Social studies-maps)

Science

Have a nurse or other medical personnel demonstrate the proper way to care for a wound, sprain, or break. When should hospital care be sought in tending the person? Explain the care and follow-up procedures that the patient must receive. (Science-health)

List the items that would be included in a first aid kit to be carried in a vehicle or kept at home for emergencies. What first aid items are carried to a fire drill? (Science-health)

Mathematics

Use the two pie-shaped graphs to answer these questions about the revenues and expenses for the American Red Cross. (Math-spatial relationships)

a. What is the biggest source of income for the Red Cross?

b. How do gifts rank in importance of income?

c. What is the smallest source of income?

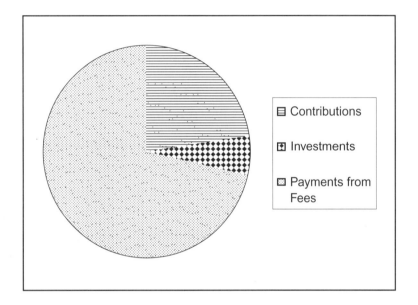

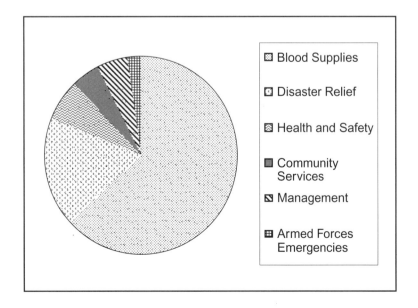

d. What is the largest expenditure area?

e. Is more money spent on community services or disaster relief?

f. What is the smallest expense area?

The American Red Cross holds blood drives in locations all over the United States. These blood drives are advertised on posters and must include the location of the drive and the time it will be held. Have students create posters to make persons aware of the blood drives. (Arts-media, Arts-visual connections)

Computer

Using the key words "Clara Barton National Historical Site," locate the Web site for this historical location. What can you learn about Clara Barton and the American Red Cross from this Web site? (English-research)

Library Media Center

Are there any Red Cross handbooks in the Library Media Center? These include information on topics such as swimming and canoeing. If no handbooks are available, inquire into obtaining some of these books. (English-sources)

Puzzle

The following words are used in the crossword puzzle:

suffragette

funding

Maryland

Europe

Johnstown

teacher

soldiers

Civil War

battlefield

REFERENCES

www.incwell.com/Biographies/Barton.html. Biographical information about Clara is given, along with other sites to investigate.
www.nps.gov/clba. This information was gathered together by the National Park Service.

Clara Barton

Across

4. Members of an army.

6. A place where fighting takes place.

7. Site of Clara Barton's home.

8. Clara Barton's first career.

9. Clara Barton aided victims of this town's flood.

Down

1. War between the states.

2. Clara Barton traveled extensively there.

3. Resources to run an organization.

5. One who works for women's voting rights.

Answer to puzzle appears on page 126.

CHAPTER 11

Dreaming of America

Written by Eve Bunting
New York: Bridge Water Books, 2000

SUMMARY

Annie Moore was in charge of her two younger brothers as they sailed from Cork, Ireland, to meet their parents in New York City. Annie was the first person to be processed at the Ellis Island facility in 1892.

RELATED CONCEPTS

Ellis Island

immigration

classes of passengers

processing

RELATED VOCABULARY

immigrant	steerage
engine	wharf
corridor	commemorate
cabin	register

ACTIVITIES

Language Arts

The inscription on the base of the Statue of Liberty is from "The New Colossus" by Emma Lazarus. Read this poem and discuss what it may have meant to the newly arrived immigrants. What does it mean to students today? (English-human experience, Social studies-world culture)

Give me your tired, your poor,
Your huddled masses yearning to breathe free,
The wretched refuse of your teeming shore.
Send these, the homeless, tempest-tossed to me
I lift my lamp beside the golden door.

Writing

Practice letter-writing skills by pretending to be someone who has immigrated to the United States and is communicating with friends or relatives "back home." (English-grammar)

Social Studies

Using information from the Library Media Center and the Internet, collect photos and stories about Ellis Island when it was a processing center for immigrants. Compare these to a description of Ellis Island National Park today. (English-research)

Do the children have ancestors who were (or are) immigrants? Make a chart to show the array of nations represented. (Social studies-world culture)

Engage the help of family members to prepare a food dish representative of their country. These may be shared with others in the class as part of a multicultural celebration. (Social studies-world culture)

Science

One of the items that was probably served at the Moore house was Irish soda bread. This biscuit does not use yeast as a leavening agent. Study the recipe and decide what causes the bread to rise. (Science-inquiry)

3 cups flour

2 tsp. baking powder

1/2 tsp. salt

1/4 cup sugar

1-1/2 cups buttermilk

2 eggs

Combine dry ingredients. Mix eggs and buttermilk, and add to dry ingredients. Mix; knead several times on floured board. Shape into a round loaf and place on a greased pan. Bake at 350 degrees for one hour; when done, the bottom will have a hollow sound when tapped.

Mathematics

The children in the story are from Cork, Ireland. Locate this city on a globe and measure how many miles it is to New York. Locate other home countries of immigrants and calculate the distance to New York. Persons coming to the United States from Asian countries probably came through a city on the western or southern coast of the United States. Calculate the distances involved here. (Math-measurement)

Make a bar graph showing the countries represented by the ancestors of the children in the class. How can these figures be interpreted? (Math-spatial)

The Arts

Immigrants sang songs of their homelands as they journeyed across the ocean to settle in a new world. Ask the music teacher to help find and perform some of these songs—e.g., "O Solo Mio" from Italy, "How Can I Leave Thee" from Germany, and "Killarney" from Ireland. (Arts-music culture)

Pretend you are meeting your family members from across the Atlantic Ocean or the Pacific Ocean today. Make a "Welcome Home" placard that will help them locate you at the airport. (Arts-media)

Computer

Students' ancestors from European countries might be located using the Internet, www.ellisisland.org. *Note*: This can be a long and intricate process. All ancestors may not be listed. (English-resources)

Library Media Center

Have the librarian or teacher read *Picnic in October* to the students. This story, by Eve Bunting, tells of an immigrant family who visits the Statue of Liberty every October. (English-human experience)

Puzzle

The following words are used in the crossword puzzle:

immigration	Statue of Liberty
New York	ship
Ireland	steerage
commemorate	Ellis Island
passenger	Atlantic

REFERENCES

Bunting, Eve. *Picnic in October*. San Diego, CA: Harcourt Brace, 1999. An Italian family celebrates the "birthday" of the Statue of Liberty every October.
www.ellisisland.com/. Information about Ellis Island is given in this entry.

www.ellisisland.org/. To search immigration records, forms are provided.

www.iaci-usa.org/anniemoore.html. Annie Moore, a fifteen-year-old girl, was the first person to be processed at Ellis Island.

www.libertystatepark.com. Contains "The New Colossus" text.

Dreaming of America

Across

1. Passenger processing was done here.

4. Remember in a special way.

6. The lowest-priced passage.

7. Homeland of the main characters.

9. A person who goes on voyage.

10. Many immigrants came here.

Down

2. Moving into another country.

3. A symbol of freedom.

5. The ocean between the United States and Europe.

8. A vessel used to cross oceans.

Answer to puzzle appears on page 127.

CHAPTER 12

John Henry

Written by Julius Lester
New York: Puffin Books, 1994

SUMMARY

Legendary strong man John Henry uses his hammer to outperform a steam drill, only to die in his attempt to help build the Big Bend Tunnel. The tale is told in countless stories and songs.

RELATED CONCEPTS

legend

physical endurance

man versus machine

competition

RELATED VOCABULARY

dignity	dynamite
indomitable	steam drill
sledgehammer	tongues of fire
crew	tunnel
boulder	tombstone

ACTIVITIES

Language Arts

Discuss different genres of literature such as folk tales and heroic myths. (English-genre)
Why do most cultures have superheroes—e.g., Spider-Man, Captain America, Superman, and Batman. Name other fictional heroes. Who are real heroes in our society? (English-diversity)

Storytelling helps to satisfy the need to pass down explanatory stories from one generation to another. Are there other ways to pass on stories today? (English-audience)

What words can be used to describe John Henry? (English-interpret)

Invent a superhero. Describe this hero, both physically and emotionally. What powers does he or she possess? Does he or she have a sidekick? Does he or she work for a particular cause— e.g., down with drugs or save the Earth? (English-human experience)

Writing

Write an episode in the life of your superhero. Be sure to use topic sentences and details, descriptive language, cause and effect, and inferences. (English-grammar)

Social Studies

John Henry takes place in West Virginia. Read a description of the landforms in this state. What were the obstacles that John and the crew faced as they cut their way across this state? How does this affect the economy of the state? (Social studies-place)

Science

To demonstrate that heavy objects exert a larger force when dropped from the same height, spread a layer of Play Doh about a half-inch thick on a table. Drop objects of varying weight but similar shapes onto the Play Doh, e.g., a ping pong ball and a golf ball. Observe the depth of the indentations that were made. Compare this to the size of the hammers that John Henry used. *Note*: The deepest indentations should be made by the largest force. (Science-motion)

Mathematics

John Henry takes place in the 1870s. Locate other legends such as Paul Bunyan and Johnny Appleseed, and date when they lived (or supposedly lived). Put these dates on a time line. What events in history were happening at the same time? Are there stories of legendary heroes who live in the twentieth- and twenty-first-century United States? How long ago did the legends exist? (Math-relations)

The Arts

Draw a picture of the superhero you have invented. Pay particular attention to how the hero moves. Include other items that the hero might utilize, e.g., automobiles and tools. (Arts-media)

There are many musical versions of the story of John Henry. Ask the music teacher to present some of these to the class. *Note*: The key words "John Henry" will produce a discography of recorded versions on the Internet. (Arts-music connections)

Computer

The Chesapeake and Ohio Railroad was being built in this story. Is the route of the railroad available on the Internet? (English-sources)

Library Media Center

Ask the library media specialist to recommend folk tales from other cultures. Compare these to American folk heroes such as Johnny Appleseed, Paul Bunyan, and Pecos Bill. (English-genre)

Puzzle

The following words are found in the crossword puzzle:

boulder

tunnel

legend

steam drill

superhero

hammer

competition

dynamite

railroad

REFERENCES

Harrison, James, and Eleanor Van Zant. *Young People's Atlas of the United States.* New York: Kingfisher, 1992. Information and photos about the state of West Virginia are provided.

Osborne, Mary Pope. *American Tall Tales.* New York: Alfred A. Knopf, 1991. Heroes in other tall tales, such as Paul Bunyan and Stormalong, are depicted.

www.ibiblio.org/john_henry/songlist.html. Various versions of the John Henry song are written down.

John Henry

Across

4. One who performs beyond the ordinary.

5. An opening made through a mountain.

6. A strong explosive.

8. A form of transportation.

9. A large rock.

Down

1. A story that explains a person.

2. A race between two persons.

3. A steam-powered device for inserting rail spikes.

7. A device for pounding.

Answer to puzzle appears on page 127.

CHAPTER 13

Snowflake Bentley

Written by Jacqueline Briggs Martin
Boston: Houghton Mifflin, 1998

SUMMARY

Snowflake Bentley dreamed of capturing the beauty of the snowflake on photographic film. Determination and patience enabled him to do this.

RELATED CONCEPTS

symmetry	crystal structure
publication	magnification
water cycle	intellectual curiosity

RELATED VOCABULARY

snowflake	photograph
painstaking	evaporate
microscope	scholars
crystal	pneumonia

ACTIVITIES

Language Arts

Study the entry about Vermont in a world almanac or a children's atlas. What do you find out about the history, size, landforms, and products of this state? What are the weather and climate like? How did this impact the work of Snowflake Bentley? (Social studies-place)

Bentley was inventive and determined. Use a thesaurus to locate other adjectives that describe him. (Social studies-inventors)

Writing

Post one-line observations about snowflakes on the bulletin board—e.g., "Snowflakes are tiny crystals." These should accompany snowflakes that have been cut out by the students. (Science-earth materials)

Bentley said that snowflakes would be his gift to the world. Do students feel he achieved his goal or not? Write a paragraph of explanation for your choice. (English-human experience)

Social Studies

Have students bring in old photographs of their family. Photos taken before 1950 would be more indicative of changes that have appeared in our culture over the years. Make an array of the photos in a display case. *Note*: Bentley lived in the late nineteenth century. (Social studies-world culture)

Science

Magnifying snowflakes was an important part of Bentley's work. Have a science teacher explain the workings of an ordinary laboratory microscope. (Science-energy)

Have the children practice taking photographs with a disposable print-film camera or with a new digital camera. Compare how the prints are processed. Which photos are more vibrant? Which photos are most versatile? What are the cost and time differentiations between the two processes? Which are more durable? (Science-technology)

Mathematics

Photos are usually processed in these sizes: 3"×5", 4"×6", 5"×7", 8"×10" and larger. Make two or three varied cutouts of each size. On a piece of 9"×12" or 16"×20" background paper, make a collage from the smaller pieces. Put a photo of each student in the middle of his or her collage. (Arts-selection, Math-spatial)

The Arts

Make a collage of snowflakes against a dark background and use this for a bulletin board display. (Arts-media, Arts-selection)

Computer

Learn about other famous photographers such as Ansel Adams, Alfred Steiglitz, Yousef Harsh, Alfred Eisenstaedt, and Margaret Bourke-White. Other early pioneers in the field of photography include George Eastman and Matthew Brady. (Social studies-inventors)

Library Media Center

Poet Robert Frost often wrote about the cold, New England winter. Locate his work entitled "Stopping by Woods on a Snowy Evening." How does this coincide with Bentley's world? (English-human experience)

Puzzle

The following words are used in the crossword puzzle:

snowflake	magnify
camera	Vermont
winter	lens
pneumonia	crystal
scholar	evaporate
photograph	

REFERENCES

Frost, Robert. *Stopping by Woods on a Snowy Evening.* Illustrated by Susan Jeffers. New York: Dutton Children's Books, 1978. A beautiful rendering of this ode to the New England winter by poet Robert Frost.

Harrison, James, and Eleanor Van Zant. *Young People's Atlas of the United States.* New York: Kingfisher, 1992. A source of information about Bentley's home state of Vermont; a map and photos are included.

www.snowflakebentley.com/. This Web site is dedicated to Bentley's life work; photos are included.

Snowflake Bentley

Across

1. A frozen droplet of water.

3. The part of the camera that focuses the image.

5. A solid shape.

6. A picture made with a camera.

8. To change from liquid to vapor.

9. A device for making photographs.

10. Home state of Snowflake Bentley.

11. To make to appear larger.

Down

2. The season when Snowflake Bentley did his work.

4. A learned person.

7. Snowflake Bentley died of this disease.

Answer to puzzle appears on page 127.

CHAPTER 14

The Legend of the Teddy Bear

Written by Frank Murphy
Chelsea, MI: Sleeping Bear Press, 2000

SUMMARY

Theodore Roosevelt demonstrated leadership for preserving the environment early in the twentieth century. He was also the inspiration for the creation of the Teddy Bear. Later, he became president of the United States.

RELATED CONCEPTS

wide-open spaces

environmental

conservation movement

RELATED VOCABULARY

symbol	adventure
wilderness	rifle
territories	cartoonist
mustache	defenseless

ACTIVITIES

Language Arts

Students are familiar with many fictional bears—e.g., Paddington Bear, Corduroy, the Three Bears, and Winnie the Pooh. Make a display of books about these bears. (Arts-selection)

Have students bring in their own special bear for a display in the classroom. A contest can be held for the oldest bear, the funniest bear, and other categories. (Arts-selection)

Writing

Write a story or a poem using one of the above fictional bears as a main character, or students may use their own special bear as the subject of their writing. (English-grammar)

Social Studies

Teddy Roosevelt pioneered the national park system. Using the world almanac, have students locate the twenty-five largest parks. (See math activity for data.) (Social studies-place, Social studies-maps)

Science

Four of the most visited parks are the Great Smoky Mountain National Park, Olympic National Park, Grand Canyon National Park, and Yosemite National Park. In small groups, have the students find more information on these parks and be able to describe the environment— e.g., the Grand Canyon is a desert region. What problems have resulted from the popularity of these and other sites? (English-cooperative learning, Science-environments)

Have the students write reports on real-life bears including the brown bear, black bear, grizzly bear, and polar bear. (English-research)

Mathematics

Select the twenty-five largest parks, which are to be located in the social studies activity. Round off the acreage size of the parks to the closest 500,000 square miles. Sequence the parks by size after locating them. Are they the most popular of the parks? (Math-numbers)

The Arts

Select one of the national parks and design a postcard to depict this place. Write a greeting on the back of the card, giving one or two facts about the park as well as your message and the receiver's address. (Arts-media)

Computer

Teddy Roosevelt National Park grew out of his Elkhorn Park. What are the amenities of this South Dakota park today? (English-sources)

Library Media Center

Books on bears can be fictional or nonfictional. Make a display area in the library for each category. Have each student select a book to share with a small group of friends, perhaps in the lower grades. (English-research)

Puzzle

The following words are used in the crossword puzzle:

wilderness	cartoonist
president	protect
adventurous	conservation
symbol	Yellowstone

REFERENCES

Bond, Michael. *A Bear Called Paddington*. Boston: Houghton Mifflin, 2001. A lovable bear is found in one of London's train stations.

Freeman, Don. *Corduroy*. New York: Puffin Books, 1976. Corduroy the Bear fears that his life will be confined to the shelf in the toy department.

Milne, A. A. *The Complete Tales of Winnie the Pooh*. New York: Dutton Books, 2001. All of the adventures of the Pooh friends are found in this volume.

http://members.aol.com/obhistory/index. Sites relevant to the boyhood of Theodore Roosevelt in Oyster Bay, NY, are given.

www.nps.gov/thro/tr_roose.htm. This is a means of accessing information on national parks.

www.us-national-park.net/. All of the U.S. national parks can be accessed by name or by state.

The Legend of the Teddy Bear

Across

4. Remote natural area.

5. Highest political office in the United States.

6. One who loves to try daring feats.

8. To keep from harm.

Down

1. First national park.

2. Wise use of natural resources.

3. Artist who draws comic strips.

7. Stands for an item or an idea.

Answer to puzzle appears on page 127.

CHAPTER **15**

Wheels in Time

Written by Catherine Courley

Brookfield, CT: Millbrook Press, 1997

SUMMARY

From childhood on, Henry Ford wanted to be a man who made things. His work with the assembly line process and interchangeable parts made automobile ownership a reality for most Americans.

RELATED CONCEPTS

horseless carriage

internal combustion engine

assembly line

interchangeable parts

RELATED VOCABULARY

machine	quadricycle
mechanic	cylinder
mainspring	Model T
contraption	production
steam engine	museum
locomotive	

ACTIVITIES

Language Arts

Most items today are made on an assembly line. However, some items are still made one at a time—e.g., designer clothes, most houses, collectible art, some autos, and handcrafted goods such as pottery. How is this manner of production reflected in the price of these items? The quality? (Social studies-trade)

Discuss how the availability of the auto transformed the society of that time. Could our society survive today if motorized transportation were no longer available? How would our way of life change? Why is it said that Americans have a love affair with their autos? Why is getting a driver's license considered to be a rite of passage? Why is the kind of car you drive a status symbol? (Social studies-rights, Science-technology and society)

Writing

Henry Ford and Thomas Edison were close friends. Have the students prepare a skit or dialog in which they theorize what the two inventors may have said to each other. (Social studies-inventors, English-audience)

Henry Ford wanted to be a mechanic and build the future. What do students see as the future of today's transportation industry? (Science-technology and society)

Social Studies

An assembly line works on the premise that each worker has one and only one job to do. As the item being made is moved along a conveyor belt, each worker does his or her task and sends the product on to the next worker. Henry Ford's assembly line refined and speeded up the process of auto production and lowered the cost of the car. This made it possible for the average American family to own an automobile. (Social studies-distribution)

Participate in a classroom assembly line process by making holiday greeting cards. Stations to be assigned include the following. (Social studies-trade)

One person to fold one 8-1/2" × 11" white paper in half to size 8-1/2" × 5-1/2".

Four persons to cut out a holiday title, a picture for the cover, an inside greeting, and an inside picture.

Four additional persons will be needed to glue each of these pieces of paper to the white folded sheet.

Additional persons will sign the cards, fold them, put them in envelopes, address them, and deliver them.

Create a timeline for the early auto industry. (Math-numbers)

Ford Motor Company can be found all over the world. On a large map, indicate where these branches of the company are located. (Social studies-maps)

Belgium	Venezuela
Switzerland	Poland
Thailand	Canada
Great Britain	Philippines

Discuss the term "globalization" in conjunction with this activity. (Social studies-nations)

Science

Before Ford invented the concept of interchangeable parts, every piece of a tool or machine had to be handmade by a craftsman. The piece would fit only that one item. Today, common interchangeable parts would include light bulbs, bicycle pedals, air filters in autos, the wheel off a toy, keys on a musical instrument, nuts and bolts, and threaded pipes. Have the students bring in an interchangeable part, and see if students can recognize its origin. (Science-technology)

Build two identical Lego structures. How can this demonstrate the theory of interchangeable parts? (Science-technology)

Mathematics

Randomly select 100 cars such as those in a parking lot. Record the colors of these cars. How many colors were represented? Make a bar graph to indicate how autos can be grouped by color. (Math-numbers)

Mark down the kinds of vehicles that make up the randomly selected vehicles—autos, SUVs, trucks, and vans. Graph these numbers to see which vehicle style is most common. (Math-numbers)

Compare the cost of buying gasoline for different vehicles of varying sizes for specified distances. (Math-relations)

Compact car averages 38 mpg—300 miles

Standard sedan averages 25 mpg—400 miles

Luxury car averages 19 mpg—200 miles

SUV averages 15 mpg—200 miles

Figure costs based on different gasoline prices—$1.99 per gallon/regular, and $2.39 per gallon/super, and $2.69 per gallon/premium.

The Arts

Use the graphs from the math activity to make a bulletin board. Cutouts of various autos can be included along with flyers from auto dealerships. (Arts-media)

Computer

Find information about the Henry Ford Museum and Deerfield Village in Michigan—e.g., locations, admission, special collections, and educational holdings. (English-sources)

Library Media Center

Have the media specialist make a display of books on different forms of transportation. (English-genre)

Puzzle

The following words are used in the crossword puzzle:

Edison	Henry Ford
handcrafted	globalization
assembly line	Deerfield
Model T	

REFERENCES

Adler, David A. *A Picture Book of Thomas Alva Edison*. New York: Holiday House, 1999. Edison was one of Ford's best friends.

Aird, Hazel. *Henry Ford: Young Man with Ideas*. New York: Aladdin Library, 1986. This is a biography of Ford for older readers.

www.hfmgv.org/exhibits/hf/default.asp. This site contains information about Ford as well as photos of an early Model T Ford.

www.si.edu/resource/foq/nnah/autohist.htm. The history of the auto is part of this Web site about the automobile museum.

Wheels in Time

Across

3. Ford's friend.

5. The museum dedicated to the work of Henry Ford.

7. To extend to the entire world.

Down

1. Founded a large motor car company.

2. Each person performs one duty in the making of an automobile.

4. It sold for $850 and was the most popular car of its era.

6. The whole item is made by one person.

Answer to puzzle appears on page 128.

CHAPTER 16

Alice Ramsey's Grand Adventure

Written by Don Brown
Boston: Houghton Mifflin, 1997

SUMMARY

After an adventurous journey of nearly two months, Alice and her three companions are the first women to drive across the United States from New York to San Francisco in 1909.

RELATED CONCEPTS

transcontinental

internal combustion engine

pneumatic tires

mechanical skills

RELATED VOCABULARY

touring car	dashboard
sponsor	wedge
headlamps	pothole
levers	brake pedal
motorist	axle
Maxwell	feat
side panels	

ACTIVITIES

Language Arts

Discuss why you think Alice was determined to make this trip. Why do people take long automobile trips today? (English-interpret)

Ask an adult to obtain some advertising folders from various automotive dealers. Review these, paying particular attention to the standard and optional features that the car has. Compare several automobiles. How does the automotive company try to convince buyers to select their car? Which ones would the students select? (English-forms)

Writing

Pretend to be Alice or one of her three friends. From what you have read, make three entries in a journal written during the journey. Students will have to use their imagination as long as it is consistent with the information in the book or other sources of that time. (English-grammar)

Social Studies

Locate Alice's route from New York to San Francisco. What cities and states did she travel through? Discuss the sights she would have seen. What hazards did she have to overcome on the trip? (Social studies-maps)

Plan a trip within the United States. The final destination should be at least 10–12 states away from the students' home. Include the following items in the report. (Social studies-place, Math-problems)

a. Distance covered (include a map)

b. Major highways followed

c. Number of days on the road

d. Cost for motels ($75.00 per day)

e. Cost for food ($30.00 per adult, $20.00 per child per day)

f. Cost for gasoline (see the math activity)

g. Attractions

h. Cost for admissions and toll roads, if known

Alice used a Blue Book, which told her which roads to take. Often, directions stated "Turn at the red barn" or "After you cross the Platte River, turn left." There were no maps and no MapQuest to help plan a trip. Write some directions from your school to your home or some other destination. Use descriptors such as Alice had in the Blue Book. (English-grammar)

Science

Potholes and ruts in the roads could be dangerous and time consuming. Using your scientific knowledge, plan how you would get Alice out of a pothole. (Science-inquiry)

Mathematics

To find the cost of gasoline for a trip, follow these steps. (Math-relations)

Take the odometer reading at the beginning of the trip when the tank is full of gasoline.

At the next filling station, write down the mileage after you fill the tank. How far did you go—e.g., 200 miles? How much gasoline did the car take—e.g., 20 gallons?

Divide the number of miles by the number of gallons—e.g., 200 divided by 20 equals 10 miles per gallon. Repeat this procedure several more times to get a consistent answer. To find the cost of the gasoline, multiply the number of gallons by the cost per gallon—e.g., $1.99 for regular, $2.39 for super, and $2.69 for premium.

If a car went 20 mph, how far would it go in 5 hours? (100 miles.) If a car went 40 mph, how far would it go in 15 hours? (525 miles.) Have the children make up other math problems using different rates of speed—e.g., 35 mph in town speed, 55 mph for highway speed, and 65 mph for limited-access highway speed. (Math-relations)

The Arts

Obtain a drivers' instruction manual. Study the various signs that signify recommended speed, traffic flow, and so on. Have the students invent a set of traffic signs for an imaginary society. (Arts-media)

Computer

On the Internet, find important dates in the history of the automobile. Place them on a time line. (English-sources, Math-numbers)

The Maxwell automobile, which Alice drove, is no longer manufactured. What happened to this early automobile company? (English-research)

Library Media Center

Can the library media specialist locate books about classic automobiles? Have a display of these books along with models of autos that students have made or purchased. (English-genre, Arts-visual connections)

Puzzle

The following words are used in the crossword puzzle:

Maxwell	pothole
accelerate	race
tire	lever
brakes	speed
axle	competition

Alice Ramsey's Grand Adventure

Across

1. A race to see who will excel.

4. A competition to see who will win an event.

5. A metal bar attached to a wheel at each end.

9. To increase speed and go faster.

10. The rate at which an automobile ran.

Down

2. Wheel covering.

3. The maker of Alice's car.

6. Iron bar that control the movement of the car.

7. Devices that stop the car.

8. A depression in the road causing damage to the tire.

Answer to puzzle appears on page 128.

REFERENCES

www.americanhistory.si.edu/onthemove/collection/object_470.html. Photos of Alice and her companions are shown.

www.Lilypadbooks.com/scstore/p-CoastC.html. Patricia Hyatt's book about Alice is for older readers.

www.Themuseumofautomobilehistory.com/. This museum about the auto is the largest of its kind.

CHAPTER 17

Fly High

Written by Louise Borden and Mary Kay Kroeger
New York: Margaret K. McElderry Books, 2001

SUMMARY

Aviatrix Bessie Coleman, a staunch worker for civil rights, fulfilled her dream to fly. Her life was cut short in an airplane accident.

RELATED CONCEPTS

aviation

aviatrix

prejudice

equal opportunity

memorial service

RELATED VOCABULARY

manicurist	cockpit
barbershop	rudder
Victrola	biplane
passport	tailspin

ACTIVITIES

Language Arts

Bessie was a role model for others. How did she earn this title? Do the students have role models—parents, other relatives, or an older friend? What makes these persons special? (English-diversity, English-interpret)

Bessie lived for some time in France. Learn some simple phrases in French to use in the classroom. (Social studies-world culture)

Bonjour.	Hello.
Au revoir.	Goodbye.
Comment vas-tu?	How are you?
Je vais bien, merci.	I am fine, thank you.
Oui/non	Yes/no
Excusez-moi.	Excuse me.
Quelle heure est il?	What time is it?
Comment t'appelles-tu?	What is your name?
S'il vous plait/Merci	Please/thank you
Je ne comprend pas français.	I do not understand French.
Monsieur, Madame, Mademoiselle	Mr./Mrs./Miss

Writing

Bessie always wanted to be "somebody." What is a "somebody"? How did she attain this goal? How could students become a somebody? Is this based on occupation, family, values, or something different? (English-research, English-grammar)

Social Studies

Bessie lived in several locations. On a globe, find Texas, Illinois, Florida, and France. Was there commercial air service between these places during Bessie's life? What forms of transportation were available at this time? (Social studies-maps)

Science

There are four forces influencing the takeoff, landing, and flight of an airplane. Lift helps the plane rise into the air, gravity pushes down on the plane, thrust pushes the plane forward, and drag causes it to slow down. What forces must be overcome to allow takeoff? What forces are involved with landing a plane? Have the teachers demonstrate these forces with a diagram or model airplane. (Science-technology)

Have the students research the lives of other aviation pioneers such as the Wright Brothers, Charles Lindberg, Glenn Curtis, Chuck Yeager, Jacqueline Cochran, Sally Ride, and Amelia Earhart. Give brief reports on these men and women. (Science-inventors)

Mathematics

An airplane often flies with a tailwind that pushes the plane ahead or a headwind that pushes against it. These winds can effectively alter the speed of the plane. For example, a plane going

200 mph with a 50 mph tailwind is actually going 250 mph. A plane going 300 mph with a 60 mph headwind is going 240 mph. Calculate the actual speed in these cases. (Math-problems)

150 mph/30 mph tailwind—180 mph

250 mph/50 mph headwind—200 mph

Make up other problems or combine facts: the plane is flying 150 mph with a headwind of 25 mph (125 mph), followed by flying 150 mph with a 15 mph tailwind (165 mph).

The Arts

The 1920s was an outstanding period in the art world. Find out about these artists and the movements with which they were associated. (Arts-appreciation)

Cubism—Pablo Picasso

Dadaism—Marcel Duchamp

Surrealism—Salvatore Dali, Max Ernst

Harlem Renaissance—William Johnson, Jacob Lawrence

Computer

Flight simulation games can be purchased at local electronic stores for about $50. See how the students would perform with the beginning instruction for flight school. (Science-technology, Science-motion)

Library Media Center

Bessie lived during a time known as the "Roaring '20s." Find a book on American history that describes this decade. (Social studies-community)

Puzzle

The math puzzle will give you an important line in the story. Find the point value for each number using the numbers in the unit for *Going West* (p. 32). Write the letters in the proper spaces under the number.

25 15 21 3 1 14 2 5 19 15 13 5 2 15 4 25. 25 15 21 3 1 14

6 12 25 8 9 7 8 10 21 19 20 12 9 11 5 13 5.

Answer

You can be somebody. You can fly high just like me.

REFERENCES

Old, Wendie C. *To Fly: The Story of the Wright Brothers*. New York: Clarion Books, 2002. This recent biography is about the first men to fly—Wilber and Orville Wright.

www.bessiecoleman.com. An extensive amount of information on Bessie can be retrieved using this site.

www.ninety-nines.org/coleman.html. Bessie Coleman was honored by the U.S. government with a commemorative postage stamp.

CHAPTER **18**

The Gardener

Written by Sarah Stewart

New York: Farrar, Straus and Giroux, 1997

SUMMARY

Lydia is sent to live in the city with her Uncle Jim during the Great Depression. Her love of plants transforms a barren roof into a garden and lifts the spirits of her family and friends.

RELATED CONCEPTS

Depression

gardening

RELATED VOCABULARY

sense of humor   bulb

window box   vacant lot

seed catalog   sprout

ACTIVITIES

Language Arts

Compare Lydia's home on the title page to the city scenes throughout the book. How are they alike and different? Which would the students choose as a place to live? Give reasons for your choice. (Social studies-community)

Writing

After Lydia returned home, she wanted to thank Uncle Jim for his kindness. Write a letter that reflects her true feelings about Uncle Jim, the friends she made, and her stay in the city. (English-grammar)

Social Studies

This story takes place during the Great Depression in the early to middle 1930s. Find out more facts about the Depression and why children were sometimes sent to live with relatives. (Social studies-resources)

The city in the story is not named. Using a world almanac, list and locate the twenty most populated cities in the United States. Are any of these cities in the students' state? If not, what are the most populous cities in that state? Select different cities to discuss their size, major attractions, economic effect, and so on. (Social studies-place)

Science

Imagine that a new plant has been discovered in the jungles surrounding the Amazon River. It will be named after the student who discovered it. To gain this honor, other botanists will expect to see drawings of the entire plant, the leaves, the stem, a bud, and a flower in full bloom. Give any known history of the plant as well as instructions for its care—e.g., amount of water and sunlight. (Science-organisms)

If it is spring, arrange to have a perennial flower swap. Gardeners who have perennial gardens can dig up plants that are too crowded. These are brought to a central location to swap for perennials from other gardeners. Or the gardeners may wish to give these flowers away to prospective gardeners. (Science-organisms)

Mathematics

Select a recipe for a cake or other baked good. Double the ingredients in the recipe. (Math-relations)

Using a seed catalog, order at least twelve flower packets to plan a flower garden. In a real flower garden, it is best to have the taller flowers in the back, and the shorter ones in front. Make a diagram showing how the seeds will be planted. This could also be done using seedlings from a garden center instead of seeds. (Science-organisms)

Low-growing plants

marigolds

English daisies

wax begonias

pansies

Medium-sized plants

coral bells

bleeding heart

chrysanthemums

sweet William

Taller plants

hollyhock

columbine

lupine

aster

The Arts

Visit a bakery to see how frosting flowers for cakes are made. What ingredients are used in the frosting? How is the frosting colored? What special tools are used? *Note*: It may be more convenient to have a cake decorator visit the classroom. (Arts-visual connections)

Computer

Seed companies from around the United States are listed on this site: http://oregonstate.edu/NWREC/seedlist.html. Are there any companies near the students? How much do seed packets cost? Does it matter which location you use when you buy seeds, bulbs, trees, and so on for a garden? (English-sources)

Library Media Center

The term "gardening" has many diverse meanings. Look in the Library Media Center for books on foliage plants, flowering plants, annuals, perennials, container gardening, and window boxes. Become familiar with these different methods of growing plants. (English-genre)

Puzzle

The following words are found in the crossword puzzle:

cakes	seeds
catalogs	flowers
Depression	uncle
Lydia	garden

REFERENCES

http://history1900s.about.com/library/photos/blygd45.htm. Photographs of the Great Depression have been archived here. Lydia spent much of her time with Uncle Jim during this time.

www.kidsgardening.com. How to start youngsters on the road to being successful gardeners; also includes attractive photos.

The Gardener

Across

2. Lydia's _____ owned the bakery.

4. The heroine of this story.

6. A collection of plants placed in an organized manner.

7. Lydia grew these colorful blossoms on the roof.

8. Uncle Jim decorated these for special occasions.

Down

1. Plants grow from these.

3. Lydia looked in these to decide which seeds to buy.

5. A period of economic decline when most people had little money.

Answer to puzzle appears on page 128.

CHAPTER **19**

Amelia and Eleanor Go for a Ride

Written by Pam Nunoz Ryan
New York: Scholastic Press, 1999

SUMMARY

First Lady Eleanor Roosevelt and aviatrix Amelia Earhart leave the formalities of a White House dinner for a flight to nearby Baltimore and back. On the flight, they discuss the need for women's rights.

RELATED CONCEPTS

independence

Secret Service

birds of a feather

RELATED VOCABULARY

outspoken   cockpit

determined   runway

daring   monuments

aviator

ACTIVITIES

Language Arts

Using a Venn diagram, discuss how Amelia and Eleanor were alike, yet different. Include topics such as their childhood, dreams, accomplishments, and other things. (Math-spatial)

Both Amelia and Eleanor were highly admired women. Why was this so? What women are highly admired today? (English-research)

The book states that Amelia and Eleanor were "birds of a feather." Other sayings to describe them are that they were "cut from the same cloth" or were "two peas in a pod." What is the meaning of these three idioms? (English-forms, English-grammar)

Eleanor Roosevelt was an outstanding first lady. What were some of her accomplishments while she lived in the White House? (English-research)

Writing

Amelia and her husband were invited to stay at the White House. Write a thank you letter to the Roosevelts from Amelia conveying their appreciation for the visit. (English-grammar)

Social Studies

The two women flew from Washington, DC, to Baltimore, Maryland. Locate these cities on a map of the DC area. How far apart are these cities? How long does it take to fly between the cities? How long does it take to drive between the cities during regular daytime traffic? (Social studies-maps)

On a street map of Washington, DC, locate the following buildings that the women saw—e.g., the White House, the Capitol building, the Washington Monument, the Smithsonian, the Lincoln Memorial, and the National Gallery of Art. With your teacher, discuss the importance of these buildings. (Social studies-place)

Science

Bernoulli's principle explains why items heavier than air, such as planes, can fly. Hold a 8-1/2" × 11" sheet of paper on two adjacent corners with the thumbs and forefingers. Blow across the top of the paper. The paper will rise in the air, indicating how the plane lifts off the ground. (Science-materials)

Mathematics

Locate the landing places by state or country where Amelia stopped during her attempted round-the-world flight. Using a globe and a measuring tape, log the distance between each stop until she took off for Howland Island. What are the total miles that she logged? The following are the places she landed after taking off from Oakland, California: (Social studies-maps, Math-measurement)

Tucson	Massawa
New Orleans	Assab
Miami	Gwadar
San Juan	Karachi
Caripito	Calcutta
Paramaribo	Akyab (today, Sittwe)
Fortaleza	Rangoon
Natal	Bangkok

St. Louis	Singapore
Dakar	Bandung
Gao	Surabaya
Fort-Lamy (today, N'Djamena)	Kupang
Al Fastir	Darwin
Khartoum	Lae

The Arts

Have the students select one of the Washington, DC, pictures found in the computer exercise. Make a sketch of this building, and use these to make a collage or bulletin board display. (Arts-visual culture)

Computer

Access the site www.greatbuildings.com on the computer. This is a source of drawings of famous buildings around the world. (English-sources)

Library Media Center

Have the library media specialist make a display of books about airplanes—from the earliest planes to jumbo jets. (English-genre)

Puzzle

The following words are used in the crossword puzzle:

license	Baltimore
Bernoulli	monuments
aviator	White House
airplane	First Lady
Washington	

REFERENCES

www.ameliaearhart.com. This is the official Amelia Earhart Web site.
www.history.navy.mil/faqs/faq3-1.htm. Frequently asked aviation questions are answered.
www.time.com/time/time100/leaders/profile/eleanor.html. Mrs. Roosevelt was considered to be one of 100 leaders in the United States at this time.
www.whitehouse.gov/history/firstladies/ae32.html. Mrs. Roosevelt's role as first lady of the country is discussed.
www.wic.org/bio/roosevel.htm. Mrs. Roosevelt's influence on the lives of others is detailed.

Amelia and Eleanor Go for a Ride

Across

1. One who flies.

4. The president's wife.

5. The principle upon which flight is based.

7. The president's house.

8. Objects or buildings to honor famous people.

Down

1. A heavier-than-air craft.

2. The capital of the United States.

3. A city near Washington.

6. A document entitling you to operate something.

Answer to puzzle appears on page 128.

CHAPTER **20**

Lou Gehrig: The Luckiest Man

Written by David A. Adler
San Diego, CA: Voyager Books, 2001

SUMMARY

Stricken by a disease that would one day bear his name, baseball player Lou Gehrig still considered himself the "luckiest man in the world."

RELATED CONCEPTS

sportsmanship

gratitude

Most Valuable Player

central nervous system

RELATED VOCABULARY

immigrants	umpire
scout	bench
signing bonus	consecutive
batting practice	Iron Horse
swing	World Series
lineup	amyotrophic lateral sclerosis
home run	teammate
baseman	appreciate

ACTIVITIES

Language Arts

Sportscasters and writers use very descriptive words as they report baseball games. In the following sentences, replace the underlined words with more high-powered ones. You may wish to use a thesaurus. (English-grammar)

The umpire said strike one.

The batter missed the ball.

The man ran to second base.

The shortstop dropped the ball.

The two fielders ran into each other.

The hot dog vender said, "Hot dogs."

The crowd stood up.

The manager spoke to the umpire.

Writing

Everyone liked Lou. How would you describe him if you were telling a younger sibling about this man? (English-human experience)

Lou Gehrig said that he was the luckiest man in the world. What does "luck" mean to you? Write a definition of this word, and include examples to prove your point. (English-grammar)

Social Studies

Lou Gehrig had a very short life, yet he accomplished many things. Give a reason why each of these dates is a milestone in his life: 1903, 1923, 1925, 1927, 1936, 1938, 1939, and 1949. These can be written as a series of news headlines. (English-research)

Locate the home cities of the teams in the two professional baseball leagues. You will need a map of the United States and Canada to mark them down. *Note*: Are there pro or semi-pro teams near the students' homes? Do the students follow the teams? (Social studies-maps)

Science

There are several variables that are related to how far a baseball will go when hit by a batter. One is the size or weight of the batter, and the other is the speed of the pitch. You can try these out during recess with a bat, ball, and tape measure to see if you can predict how far a batted ball will go. (Science-motion)

Mathematics

Use your knowledge of the baseball stadium to answer these questions. Make up additional questions for your classmates. (Math-spatial)

How many feet is it between home plate and first (90 ft.), first and second (90 ft.), second and third (90 ft.), and third and home plate (90 ft.)?

What is the distance between home plate and the pitcher's mound (60.5 ft.)?

How far does a runner travel to gain a double (180 ft.)?

How far does the runner travel to gain a triple (270 ft.)? A home run (360 ft.)?

How far is the center field fence (approximately 400 ft.)?

Box scores tell the baseball fan what each player has done in the game. Check these scores on the sports page of the newspaper. Select a player and see how many times he was at bat and how many times he had a hit. For example, a player is at bat four times. He gets one hit. That means that the player gets a hit 25 percent of the time or he is batting .250. Make up other examples to practice your knowledge of percentages. (Math-relations)

The Arts

Have a teacher or parent teach the students the melody of the song called "Take Me Out to the Baseball." Do these words fit only baseball games, or can they be transferred to other sports? (Arts-voice)

Take me out to the ballgame,
Take me out with the crowd,
Buy me some peanuts and crackerjacks,
I don't care if we ever get back,
For it's root, root, root for the home team,
If they don't win it's a shame,
For it's one, two, three strikes you're out,
At the old ball game.

Since the very early days of baseball, teams have worn an emblem on their uniforms. This signifies their team. Invent a team and design its logo. This should emphasize the city and the name of the team. (Arts-media)

The sixth grade baseball team at your school has won the city championship. How would the rest of the school honor these boys and girls, coaches, and others? A certificate might be one idea. Who would design this? (Arts-media)

Computer

There are many entries on the Internet about the National Baseball Hall of Fame in Cooperstown, NY. Which players have been inducted since the children were born? Who are some of their other favorite players? Are there newspaper articles on the Internet about Lou Gehrig and the Hall of Fame? (English-sources)

Library Media Center

In the Library Media Center, look for additional books about Lou and his best friend, Babe Ruth. Why are Lou and Babe still considered two of the best players of all time? (English-genre)

Some students may also wish to read baseball fiction by such authors as Matt Christopher. (English-genre)

Puzzle

The following words in the story are scrambled:

bunt	foul ball
triple	umpire
safe	dugout
home run	plate
ball	shortstop
pitcher	bat
runner	catcher
out	

These are the scrambled words:

crehcat	potsshrto
tuo	thipcer
preimu	tab
petal	renurn
pelrit	tugdou
luof labl	labl
meoh nur	tnub
eafs	

REFERENCES

Burleigh, Robert. *Home Run: The Story of Babe Ruth.* New York: Voyager, 2003. Babe and Lou were equally outstanding players and best friends.

Thayer, Ernest Lawrence. *Casey at the Bat.* Illustrated by Christopher Bing. Brooklyn, NY: Handprint Books, 2002. A newly illustrated version of the old poem about ballplayer Casey at the bat.

www.ballparksofbaseball.com/al/Yankeestadium.htm. Yankee Stadium has been the home of many pennant-winning teams.

www.baseballhalloffame.org/. The Baseball Hall of Fame is in Cooperstown, NY.

www.baseballhalloffame.org/hofers_and_honorees/hofer_bios/gehrig_lou.htm. Names of Hall of Famers are listed. This includes Ruth and Gehrig.

CHAPTER 21

A Picture Book of Dwight David Eisenhower

Written by David A. Adler
New York: Holiday House, 2002

SUMMARY

Sports and the study of history were an integral part of Dwight Eisenhower's life. Both would prepare him for a life as a military leader as well as a political leader who influenced much of the twentieth century.

RELATED CONCEPTS

Cold War

superpower

globalism

RELATED VOCABULARY

Allied troops	liberation
military installation	surrender
supreme command	North Atlantic Treaty Organization (NATO)
English Channel	

ACTIVITIES

Language Arts

Eisenhower was a strong military and political figure because he had proven himself to be an outstanding leader. What are the qualities that make a leader truly great, whether it is at the elementary school level or as the political leader of a large nation? Must leaders possess outgoing personalities? Should leaders delegate authority or personally see that every task is completed? Can students be trained to be leaders? (English-research)

Make a concept map showing the outstanding character traits that Eisenhower possessed. (English-research)

Writing

Due to health reasons, Eisenhower was forced to miss a year of school, which was a great disappointment to him. Have the students describe a time when they were disappointed or hypothesize a situation that could cause great disappointment. (English-grammar)

After reading this book, write down several reasons why Eisenhower is considered to be an outstanding role model. (English-human experience)

Social Studies

Eisenhower served his country in many locations around the world. Use blue ink to identify these locations. (Social Studies-maps)

The Philippines

England

France

North Africa

Panama

Using red ink, locate these places that were considered to be "hot spots" during Eisenhower's terms of office. (Social Studies-maps)

Korea	Lebanon
Hungary	Cuba
Suez	Little Rock, Arkansas

Many public schools were named after Eisenhower. Give reasons for this honor. What should all students learn about this man? (Social studies-community)

Science

Scientific research was done during Eisenhower's term of office as a part of a project called the International Geophysical Year (IGY). What were the objectives of these scientists? Have their questions been answered in the intervening years? What problems have not been resolved? (Science-earth materials)

Mathematics

Using the data given below, answer the questions about the two Eisenhower elections. (Math-questioning)

1952 Popular Vote

Eisenhower 33,036,252

Stevenson 27,313,992

1956 Popular Vote

Eisenhower 35,585,316

Stevenson   26,031,322

Round off the numbers to the nearest million. How many more votes did Eisenhower receive in 1952? (33 million, or 33,000,000.) In 1956? (35 million, or 35,000,000.) Using a world almanac for subsequent U.S. presidential elections, find out the number of votes received by each winner. Make graphs to show the comparisons.

The Arts

Be a member of Ike's reelection campaign. Design a poster that could be used for distribution by his staff. Decorate the room with these posters, banners, lapel buttons, car bumper stickers, and so on. (Arts-media)

Computer

Locate informational materials on the service academies—West Point (NY), Annapolis (MD), the Air Force Academy (CO), and the Coast Guard Academy (CT). Choose one of these academies and write a letter of application. Before you start writing, be sure to list the topics you must cover, and how you can apply your accomplishments to these school's requirements. (English-sources)

Library Media Center

Construct a bulletin board about Eisenhower using copies of photos from library sources. (English-sources)

Puzzle

The following words are used in the crossword puzzle:

Allies	West Point
Normandy	general
I Like Ike	president
history	Columbia
Mamie	Gettysburg

A Picture Book of Dwight David Eisenhower

Across

2. Eisenhower's wife.

3. Military academy that educates army officers.

5. The highest political office in the United States.

9. Countries that fight on the same side during a war.

10. Town in Pennsylvania where the Eisenhowers retired.

Down

1. The study of the past.

4. A political slogan in favor of Eisenhower.

6. A province of France.

7. The university where Eisenhower served as president.

8. The top-ranking military officer.

Answer to puzzle appears on page 129.

REFERENCES

www.dwightdeisenhower.com. More biographical information is provided.

www.eisenhowerbirthplace.org/. These are photos of his first home.

www.nps.gov/eise. The Eisenhowers retired to their Gettysburg farm.

www.whitehouse.gov/history/presidents/de34.html. Biographical information about Eisenhower is given.

CHAPTER 22

Duke Ellington: The Piano Prince and His Orchestra

Written by Andrea Davis Pinkney
New York: Scholastic, 1998

SUMMARY

Pianist Edward Kennedy ("Duke") Ellington, who became a leader of the jazz movement, wrote compositions for both classical and popular tastes. He is still considered to be one of the giants of the Golden Age of Jazz.

RELATED CONCEPTS

jazz

honky-tonk

Renaissance

cutting a rug

RELATED VOCABULARY

rhythm	blues
ragtime	orchestra
melodies	improvise
pearlies	maestro
gig	

ACTIVITIES

Language Arts

The hundredth anniversary of Duke Ellington's birth was widely celebrated in musical circles. Why was he so remembered and honored? (English-human experience, Arts-musical forms)

Writing

Listen to two very different pieces from the Duke Ellington repertoire—e.g., "Satin Doll" and "The A Train." Compare the tempos and rhythms of these two pieces. Listen to other great hits such as "Don't Get around Much Any More," "Mood Indigo," and "It Don't Mean a Thing." Do they resemble either of the first two songs? How are they different? Write down how they make you feel. (Art-musical forms)

Social Studies

Many jazz artists got their start in a section of New York City called Harlem. Locate this area on a street map of New York. Harlem today is going through a growth phase and has become much more in the spotlight. What does this growth period mean to the people who live in Harlem? (Social studies-place, Social studies-environment)

Science

Sound is produced by vibration—e.g., striking a wooden hammer against the strings of a piano. Other sounds are made by drawing a bow across a violin string, plucking guitar strings, striking percussive instruments, and blowing into the reed of a clarinet or the metal mouthpiece of a brass instrument. How else can you produce sound using vibrations? (Science-energy)

Mathematics

Listen to some of Ellington's songs. Clap the rhythms along with the music. (Math-numbers)

The Arts

Jazz was an extension of the ragtime music popular at the turn of the twentieth century. Listen to some ragtime music, and write down your reaction. (Art-musical forms)

Some of the best-known jazz artists include Louis Armstrong, Benny Goodman, Count Basie, Billie Holliday, Ella Fitzgerald, Dizzy Gillespie, Charlie Parker, John Coltrane, Dave Brubeck, and Miles Davis. These artists were very popular in the 1930s, 1940s, and 1950s but are still considered to be leaders in the field of jazz. Listen to their music. (Arts-musical forms, Social studies-environment)

Such artists as Wynton Marsalis and Cassandra Wilson earmark modern jazz. Listen to contemporary jazz and compare it to the Golden Age of Jazz. (Arts-musical forms)

Jazz music usually features a piano, drums, saxophones, trumpets, trombones, and clarinets in various combinations. Single players were acknowledged with an improvised solo. Distinguish the sounds of these instruments as they play. (Arts-instruments)

As mentioned, different band members will "improvise" or play music that has not been written down. One form of this improvisation is "scat" singing. Ask the music teacher to demonstrate these two musical forms. (Arts-improvise)

Computer

The official Web site for this hero is *www.dukeellington.com*. What kind of information does this Web site give the reader? How would this Web site be of use to the researcher? (English-sources)

Library Media Center

The Harlem Renaissance refers to a time when people in Harlem were leaders in music as well as literature and art. Find out more about the role of the Harlem Renaissance in American history—e.g., locate works by poets Langston Hughes and Paul Laurence Dunbar. (English-research)

Puzzle

The following words in the story are scrambled:

clarinet	piano
trombone	double bass
trumpet	tenor saxophone
alto saxophone	percussion

These are the scrambled words:

espionucsr	brotmoen
ubedol sabs	apion
ronte xehosaopn	tencrlai
prutmet	tola xsopneaoh

REFERENCES

Isadora, Rachel. *Bring on That Beat*. New York: G. P. Putnam's and Sons, 2002. This is a fictional book showing various aspects of the "beat" scene.

Winter, Jonah. *Once upon a Time in Chicago*. New York: Hyperion Books, 2000. Clarinetist Benny Goodman is the central character in this book.

www.Redhotjazz.com/duke.html. Ellington's monumental discography is provided.

CHAPTER 23

If a Bus Could Talk: The Story of Rosa Parks

Written by Faith Ringgold
New York: Simon & Schuster Books for Young Readers, 1999

SUMMARY

A young girl hears the story of Civil Rights activist Rosa Parks. Ms. Parks sparked the movement toward racial equality by sitting in the white-race-only section of a city bus in Montgomery, Alabama.

RELATED CONCEPTS

Civil Rights movement

Ku Klux Klan

National Association for the Advancement of Colored People (NAACP)

voter registration

RELATED VOCABULARY

segregation	Supreme Court
activist	register to vote
arrest	tribute
boycott	

ACTIVITIES

Language Arts

Produce a skit based on the life of Rosa Parks. Make hats to depict the various characters in her life. (English-audience)

Why was a street renamed "Rosa Parks Boulevard"? (English-research)

Parents and grandparents may remember events of the Civil Rights movement. Have the students interview these relatives and share what they learned. Are there others in the community who could relate some of the events from the 1950s until today? (English-research)

This book reads somewhat like the Magic School Bus series—e.g., relaying factual information in story form. Do students like this style of writing? Is it effective as a means of teaching? (English-genre)

Writing

Write a newspaper article describing one of the events in the life of Rosa Parks. Remember to answer the questions "Who?" "What?" "When?" "Where?" and "Why?" in the first paragraph of the article. Subsequent paragraphs should include pertinent details. (English-grammar)

Social Studies

On a map of Alabama, locate Selma and Montgomery. Both cities played important roles in the Civil Rights movement. This map could be part of a bulletin board display of Rosa Parks's life. (Social studies-maps)

Science

Many people argue today that workers should ride busses to cut down on pollution. Others insist that busses are major contributors to pollution. Use environmental education sources to make a statement about this controversy. Which alternative is more desirable? (Science-technology and society)

Mathematics

Here is a bus fare schedule. (Math-relations)

Adults	$1.00
Child 6–10	.50
Transfer	.10
Child under 6	free
Over 65	free

Note: Each ticket holder pays the transfer fee.
To test math skills, make up examples using these figures.

a. A mother and her two children, ages four and six, wish to go to the zoo. It will involve one transfer to get there. How much will she need to pay to get to the zoo? The cost of the return trip will be the same. What is the round-trip cost? ($3.40)

b. A sixty-six-year-old man wishes to take his five-year-old grandson to the park. How much will it cost them each way? (No charge.)

c. A twelve-year-old girl is taking her eight-year-old sister to the mall. How much will it cost them for a round trip? ($3.00)

The Arts

Many hundreds of persons joined in the boycott of the Montgomery transit system. Placards were carried as part of this protest. Create a placard advocating this boycott. (Arts-media)

Computer

On a time line of the period from 1950 to the present, indicate the names and accomplishments of the leaders who fought for civil rights—e.g., Martin Luther King, Jr., and Medgar Evers. A source of information, besides the Internet and a world almanac, is the teacher supply store, especially for Black History Month in February. (Math-numbers)

What are the facts about Rosa Parks's life after the end of the boycott against the bus company? Is she considered to be a leader in the Civil Rights movement? What were her other accomplishments? (English-research)

Library Media Center

Many talented writers today are of African American descent. Ask the media specialist to pull some of these authors' books from the shelves so that students may become familiar with them. Especially readable are writers like Langston Hughes and Paul Dunbar. (English-diversity)

Use a graphic organizer to help recall the events of the story. (English-interpret)

Problem	Event
Event	Event
Event	Solution

Puzzle

The following words are used in the crossword puzzle:

civil rights	activist
boycott	register
Alabama	Supreme Court
segregation	NAACP
integration	vote

If a Bus Could Talk: The Story of Rosa Parks

Across

4. Keeping people separate by race.

5. One who takes part in a cause.

7. The highest court in the United States.

9. Its state capital is Montgomery.

10. The privileges due to all citizens.

Down

1. To make a choice for a political candidate.

2. To sign up to vote.

3. To refuse to buy, ride, or participate.

6. To bring people of different races together.

8. The National Association for the Advancement of Colored People.

Answer to puzzle appears on page 129.

REFERENCES

Rappaport, Doreen. *Martin's Big Words: The Life of Dr. Martin Luther King.* New York: Hyperion Books, 2001. This is a recent biography of Dr. King.

http://teacher.scholastic.com/rosa/. Information on "how I fought for civil rights" and an interview with Mrs. Parks tell much about this leader.

www.tsum.edu/museum/. Information and photos are given for the Rosa Parks Library and Museum.

CHAPTER 24

Grandma's Records

Written by Eric Velazquez

New York: Walker and Company, 2001

SUMMARY

A young boy spends the summer living with his grandmother and sharing her love of music. The outstanding event of the summer was a concert by Rafael Cortijo and his band.

RELATED CONCEPTS

memories

"Elena's Candy"

RELATED VOCABULARY

nephew	albums
conga	CDs
el barrio	nightclub
merengue	concert
salsa	theater

ACTIVITIES

Language Arts

People collect phonograph records of all kinds. Some specialize in old 78 rpm disks. Invite a collector to discuss and demonstrate the music on these records. What is the difference between the sound of these records and those of a modern CD? How is the music different from music of today? (Arts-musical forms)

The boy in the story was very excited about going to his grandmother's for the summer. How do the students spend their summer—e.g., at home with their parents? With a sitter? With relatives? Or at camp? (English-research)

Writing

If Grandma writes to a relative in Puerto Rico about the concert, what would she say? Include events from the entire evening. (English-grammar)

Social Studies

Locate Puerto Rico and the Dominican Republic. (Social studies-maps)

Science

Thomas Edison invented the phonograph. Learn more about this invention and how the recording industry has changed in the last century. (Social studies-inventors, Science-technology)

Mathematics

Phonograph records are known by the speed with which they turn—78 rpm, 45 rpm, and 33.3 rpm. How many turns would each record make in the following amounts of time? (Math-relations)

1 minute (78, 45, and 33.3 turns)

3 minutes (234, 135, and 100 turns)

20 seconds (26, 15, and 11.1 turns)

Make additional problems.

The Arts

Newspapers and magazines often list the "Top Ten" singles and albums. The music may be categorized as pop, country, Latin, and rhythm and blues. Listen to samples of each.
Take a survey of the class to see which music is most popular. (Arts-musical forms)
Look at old album covers. What do they tell you about the music on the record? What can you learn about the culture of the time? Design a CD cover for a group you like, or invent your own group and design a CD cover for them. (Arts-music selection)
Can anyone demonstrate the merengue or other dances known in Puerto Rico? (Art-music culture)

Computer

Rafael Cortijo and Ismael Rivera were giants in the field of Latin music. Locate Web sites about these two men. (English-sources)

Library Media Center

If you were to visit Puerto Rico or the Dominican Republic as a tourist, what would you expect to see? (English-research)

Puzzle

The following words are found in the crossword puzzle:

albums	nephew
concert	Puerto Rico
el barrio	salsa
homesick	theatre
merengue	

REFERENCES

Juntos Otra Vez: Cortijo y su Combo con Ismael Rivera. CD, 1997. This is a CD that can be played to hear authentic Puerto Rican music.

www.musicofpuertorico.com/en/rafael_cortijo.html. Biographical information, photos, and instruments are all given in this Web site.

www.salsaweb.com/. The world's largest online salsa magazine is best for older readers.

Grandma's Records

Across

1. The relative of Grandma who also loved salsa music.

3. Island where Grandma came from.

5. Grandma felt this way about Puerto Rico.

8. A place where performances are held.

9. Another name for old phonograph recordings.

Down

2. A place in the city where Latino people live.

4. A performance.

6. A Latino dance.

7. A general name for Latino music.

Answer to puzzle appears on page 129.

CHAPTER **25**

Wilma Unlimited: How Wilma Rudolph Became the World's Fastest Woman

Written by Kathleen Krull

San Diego, CA: Voyager Books, 1996

SUMMARY

Despite several physical threats to her health and well-being, Wilma overcame immense obstacles to walk and then to run. She became a star runner in the 1960 Olympics.

RELATED CONCEPTS

segregation

competition

determination

perseverance

RELATED VOCABULARY

polio	Olympics
scarlet fever	relay
paralyze	meter
brace	baton

ACTIVITIES

Language Arts

What attributes gave Wilma the determination to fulfill her dreams? Were there other persons who helped her? What dreams do the students have for their futures? (English-diversity)

Students may not be familiar with the Olympic games. Discuss several of the summer and winter events that take place at these games—e.g., track and field, swimming and diving, the marathon, skiing, bobsledding, and ice skating. These could be pantomimed. (English-research)

Writing

Have the students define "determination" with a line poem. Each student contributes a line—e.g., "Determination is knowing you can do it." (English-grammar)

When Wilma returned to Clarksville, Tennessee, her friends and neighbors greeted her. Write a speech of commendation that would honor her. (English-audience)

Social Studies

Have students locate the sites for the summer and winter Olympics that have been held since their birth. Where did Wilma win her medals? What future sites have already been selected? Locate these cities on a world map. (Social studies-maps)

Science

Time records set by Olympic athletes are continually being broken. Why is it that people are faster and stronger today? You may wish to consult a health text to help answer this question. (Math-problem)

As a child, Wilma had polio. This dread disease has been nearly eradicated from the earth through the work of dedicated men and women in a service group known as Rotary International. Invite a Rotarian to speak about this humanitarian task, which has inoculated over 1 billion children since its inception. (Social studies-world culture)

For many years, the possibility of a polio epidemic was greatly feared by parents. Young children seemed particularly susceptible to the disease, and they were kept from crowded places such as swimming pools and movies. What were the effects of polio that caused such fear? (Science-health)

Mathematics

On the playground, measure out 100 meters, 200 meters, and 400 meters—the events Wilma ran. Compare these distances to other objects that the students know—e.g., the classroom, the gymnasium, and the distance to the fire drill gathering place. (Math-measurement, Math-questioning)

Ask children to volunteer to run these distances. Time them and compare the scores to Wilma's. If possible, find out what the record scores are for high school track and field events, and compare them to Wilma's records. (Math-measurement, Math-questioning)

The Arts

At each Olympics, the team from every country wears a special outfit. Design a jacket for the upcoming Olympics. The five interlocking rings, which are the symbol of the games, may give students ideas. (Arts-selection, Arts-media)

Computer

A vaccine to immunize people against polio was developed by Jonas Salk. Louis Sabin later developed an oral form of the vaccine. Find out more about the work of these two men. (Social studies-inventors)

Library Media Center

Locate a book on medical pioneers. Learn about men and women who have made our lives better through their research. (Social studies-inventors)

Puzzle

These are the words for the crossword puzzle:

Rome	competition
polio	Olympics
records	relay
meter	baton
immunize	field and track

REFERENCES

www.gardenofpraise.com/ibdwilma.htm. This site gives a biography and photo of Wilma.
www.lkwdpl.org/wihohio/rudo-wil.htm. This site also has a biographical sketch of Wilma.

Across

4. A race where a baton is passed from one runner to another.

5. The fastest or best time set in an athletic competition.

6. A race or contest.

8. A unit of measurement slightly larger than one yard.

9. The marker used in a relay race.

10. The site of the 1960 Olympics.

Down

1. Athletic competitions consisting of running and jumping events.

2. A childhood disease that Wilma contracted.

3. International athletic competition held every four years.

7. To administer vaccine to prevent disease.

Answer to puzzle appears on page 129.

CHAPTER 26

Harvesting Hope: The Story of Cesar Chavez

Written by Kathleen Krull

San Diego, CA: Harcourt, 2003

SUMMARY

Seeing the pitiful conditions of migrant workers, Chavez agitated for farm reform. He became the cofounder of the United Farm Workers (UFW) and led the way to better working conditions.

RELATED CONCEPTS

organizers

justice

fighter

nonviolence

"La Causa"

contract

RELATED VOCABULARY

fiesta

barbecue

adobe

ranch

migrant workers

graduation

compassionate

National Farm Workers Association (NFWA)

strike

march

obstacle

ACTIVITIES

Language Arts

The Chavez family lost their ranch in Arizona because of a drought. They were then forced to become migrant workers in California. Discuss the economic struggle that resulted from this chain of events. How did the lives of the family members change? How did it affect the life of Cesar Chavez? (English-research, Social studies-migration)

Storytelling was very important to the lives of the workers. Why do people often prefer to hear information in story form? How do families use the idea of storytelling to impart knowledge? Have the students tell brief stories about their lives or their family. (English-genre)

There are many causes today for which people participate in marches—e.g., multiple sclerosis and heart disease. Ask someone who is involved in one of these marches to talk about the goals of the march and what is accomplished—e.g., fund-raising and information dispersal. (English-research)

Writing

Both Cesar Chavez and his colleague Dolores Huerta have received humanitarian awards over the years. Write a biography of one of these persons indicating the reasons why they were chosen for these awards. (English-grammar)

Make a concept map about Cesar Chavez. His life can be broken into three sections—his childhood in Arizona, the early years as a migrant worker, and the period of "Viva la Causa," "Long Live the Cause," the movement for social change *or* social justice for farm workers begun by Chavez. (English-interpret)

There is much controversy over the speaking of English in the United States. Some people feel that all persons from another culture should learn English as soon as possible. Others feel that the native language should be retained as a primary vehicle of communication. Ask for volunteers to defend these two opinions in a class debate. Those not included in the actual debate can vote for the side that has the best argument. (English-audience)

Social Studies

On a detailed map of California, locate places important to Chavez—e.g., Fresno, Delano, Sacramento, Modesto, and Stockton. (Social studies-maps)

Science

Select several foods that are harvested by migrant workers and display them on a poster. What nutritional value do these foods have—e.g., vitamins, fiber, and calcium? (Social studies-distribution)

Using the monthly precipitation and temperature chart in a world almanac, graph these figures for each month in Fresno, California. What do you learn about the climate in this agricultural center? (Science-natural resources)

Mathematics

Hispanics are now the largest minority group in the United States. Using an almanac or information from the Internet, find other groups that are included in population statistics. Make a graph showing the number of persons representing each culture. *Note*: The largest number on the vertical axis will be 40,000,000 persons. (English-sources)

The Arts

Make posters expressing the feelings of those who participated in the march to Sacramento. How did the workers hope to bring others to believe in their cause? (Arts-media)

Computer

Find information on the Internet about the cities listed in the social studies activity. What is the economic base in this area? Are migrant workers still important to the area? (Social studies-place)

Library Media Center

Ask the library media specialist to locate other books about children of migrant workers—e.g., *Tomas and the Library Lady* and *Working Cotton*. Are there other books on this topic? (English-genre)

Puzzle

The following words are found in the crossword puzzle:

Hispanic	march
Fresno	Arizona
vegetables	Chavez
Sacramento	Huerta

REFERENCES

Ryan, Pam Munoz. *Esperanza Rising*. New York: Scholastic, 2000. Esperanza's family loses their land, much like the Chavez family did.

Williams, Sherley Anne. *Working Cotton*. San Diego, CA: Harcourt Brace Jovanovich, 1992. A day in the life of a migrant worker child is featured.

www.incwell.com/Biographies/Chavez.html. This is a biography of Chavez.

www.ufw.org/history.htm. Biographies of Chavez and other UFW leaders, photos of Chavez, and other sites to click on are sponsored by the United Farm Workers.

Across

4. Person of Spanish-speaking background.

6. Chavez's colleague and cofounder of the UFW.

7. Capital of California.

Down

1. Demonstrators marched through this city.

2. To participate in a walking demonstration.

3. Migrant workers picked these.

5. Chavez's home state.

8. He preached nonviolence as a way of making change.

Answer to puzzle appears on page 130.

One Giant Leap: The Story of Neil Armstrong

Written by Don Brown
Boston: Houghton Mifflin, 1998

SUMMARY

All his life, Neil Armstrong dreamed of a career in the aviation industry. Eventually, he achieved this goal and became the first man to walk on the moon.

RELATED CONCEPTS

    test pilot

    manned spacecraft

    gravity

RELATED VOCABULARY

propeller	hover
bank	orbit
figure 8	telescope
astronaut	Saturn rocket
spacecraft	

ACTIVITIES

Language Arts

Certain events in history are marked on the memories of those who witnessed them. Ask friends or relatives where they were or what they were doing when men first landed on the moon—July 20, 1969. (English-research)

Why are astronauts considered to be heroes? Is it their training? Their knowledge? Their determination? Their accomplishments in space? Are there other reasons? (Social studies-inventors)

Writing

Write a paragraph describing the first airplane flight that you took or an anticipated flight you would like to take. (English-grammar)

Social Studies

Ohio is called the birthplace of aviation. Locate the Wright brothers' home in Dayton and Armstrong's home in Wapakoneta, Ohio. How is this reflected in the design of the Ohio state quarter? What other quarter honors the Wright Brothers? Other places famous in the field of aviation and rocketry include Kitty Hawk, North Carolina; Houston, Texas; and Cape Kennedy, Florida. (Social studies-maps)

Make a time line of the history of manned space flight. Include achievements as well as setbacks. (Math-numbers)

Have the students present short reports on other aviation pioneers such as the Wright Brothers, Charles Lindberg, Glenn Curtis, Chuck Yeager, Amelia Earhart, Jacqueline Cochran, Bessie Coleman, and Sally Ride. (Social studies-inventors)

Science

What advances have been made in our knowledge of outer space since Armstrong walked on the moon? What problems do scientists face today? Is it advantageous to resume manned flights to the moon or to continue keeping the flights on hold? Will exploratory trips such as the Mars Rover be beneficial to humankind? (Science-universe)

Mathematics

Observe and draw a sketch of the moon every four or five days for one month. What phenomenon was recorded? Using students to represent the sun, the moon, and the earth, pantomime the revolutions of the moon and the earth. Solar and lunar eclipses can also be depicted. (Math-spatial)

The Arts

Collect photos and articles about the July 20, 1969, landing on the moon. Make a collage from these for a bulletin board. (Arts-media, English-sources)

Design a computer mouse pad related to this story. (Arts-media)

Computer

A great many teaching aids can be found on the Internet at www1.nasa.gov/home, which is the home page for the National Aeronautic and Space Administration (NASA).

Library Media Center

Check encyclopedia yearbooks or recently copyrighted encyclopedias to learn more about the 1969 moon landing. The library media specialist may have other books on this topic. (English-research)

Puzzle

Each number in the statement has a corresponding letter. When letters have been filled in beneath each number, you will have an important line in the story. Use the chart in the puzzle section of the chapter for *Going West* (p. 32) to help you.

Neil Armstrong spoke this statement to the whole world as he stepped onto the moon's surface.

20 8 1 20' 19   15 14 5   19 13 1 12 12   19 20 5 16   6 15 18   13 1 14,

15 14 5   7 9 1 14 20   12 5 1 16   6 15 18   13 1 14 11 9 14 4

Answer

That's one small step for man, one giant leap for mankind.

REFERENCES

http://mars.jpl.nasa.gov/mer/. Information about the Mars Expedition Rover can be accessed at this site.

www.jpl.nasa.gov/kids. The new and improved "Space Place" offers many activities for schoolchildren.

www.nasa.gov/audience/forkids/. All types of information on outer space can be retrieved from this and the previous NASA sites.

CHAPTER 28

Oh, the Places He Went

Written by Maryann Weidt

Minneapolis, MN: Carolrhoda Books, 1994

SUMMARY

Animals and their movement always fascinated Theodore Geisel. As Dr. Seuss, his artistic ability enabled him to create magical characters in a fantastic world loved by children and adults.

RELATED CONCEPTS

fantasy

imagination

inspiration

word play

RELATED VOCABULARY

volunteer	"bone pile"
pneumonia	critic
shy	edit
artist	manuscript
cartoon	doctorate

ACTIVITIES

Language Arts

Invent a Seuss-like critter. Give the animal a name, and describe its physical features and personality—e.g., disposition, food preferences, habitat, and likes and dislikes. (Arts-media, Arts-selection)

Celebrate Dr. Seuss's birth date—March 2, 1904. Plan a day based on Seuss books, which can be read to classes by teachers, principals, local officials, law enforcement persons, parents, and/or high school students. Students can wear Cat in the Hat headgear, costumes, pins, banners, sandwich boards—anything to honor Dr. Seuss. Teachers may wish to include skits depicting specific books, crosswords, and other puzzles based on Seuss works. (English-human experience)

Writing

Write an adventure story starring your critter. (English-grammar)

Dr. Seuss knew the secret of writing children's books. Have the students list three reasons why they think Dr. Seuss was so successful in his work. Discuss these ideas. (English-forms)

Social Studies

Dr. Seuss wrote about the places you can go. Have the students select a place they would like to go and write about it. These places can be put on a map. (Social studies-place, English-grammar)

Make a bulletin board display with small drawings to represent "geographical places" in Dr. Seuss books. This could also become a game board. (Arts-selection, Arts-visual connection)

Science

Draw a picture of the environment in which your critter lives—e.g., the seashore, a deep forest, a river valley, or mountains. (Science-environment)

Mathematics

Write a counting book using your Seuss critter as the main character. The book may show number counting from one to ten or backwards from ten to one. Or numbers may be counted by twos, fives, or tens. The counting book may or may not be rhymed, but should lend itself to repetition and rhythm so that students will enjoy reading it. (Math-numbers)

The Arts

Draw a picture of the critter you invented above. Show the critter at rest and engaged in some activity. (Arts-media)

Design a Dr. Seuss lunchbox or backpack. (Arts-selection)

Computer

Find a Dr. Seuss fan club on the Internet. What can you learn from this? Or form your own fan club. (English-sources)

Library Media Center

Have the library media specialist make a display of all the Dr. Seuss books in the center. Let each student in the class or school vote for his or her favorite book. Tally these choices to find the winner and runners up. These can be put on a bar graph. (English-genre)

Puzzle

The following words are found in the crossword puzzle:

Academy award	Hop on Pop
Cat in the Hat	Horton
green eggs and ham	Lorax
fish	Oobleck
Geisel	places

REFERENCES

www.catinthehat.org/. Here is information about the Dr. Seuss Memorial in Massachusetts.
www.nea.org/readacross/. "Read across America" activities are given.
www.todayinliterature.com/biography/theodor.seuss.geisel.asp#books_by. This bibliography features all of Dr. Seuss's books.

Oh, the Places He Went

Across

4. A very kind elephant.

6. Dr. Seuss's real name.

7. One _____ Two _____ .

8. Oh, the _____ He Went.

10. Highest honor in the motion picture industry.

Down

1. A strange breakfast dish.

2. Who to hop on.

3. The Seuss's lovable feline.

5. Gooey stuff.

9. He speaks for the trees.

Answer to puzzle appears on page 130.

CHAPTER 29

The Wall

Written by Eve Bunting
New York: Clarion Books, 1990

SUMMARY

A father takes his young son to see the name of his grandfather on the Vietnam War Memorial. Others in the area also pay their respects to the dead.

RELATED CONCEPTS

memorial

RELATED VOCABULARY

soldier

medals

remembrance

rubbings

ACTIVITIES

Language Arts

Students can honor those in the military who have died for their country and those who are veterans. An assembly for the entire school can be organized for a Memorial Day observation or for Veterans Day. Here is a program given on Veterans Day. (English-audience)

Posting the colors: Boy Scout Troup

Pledge to the flag: President, Student Council

National anthem: Combined boys and girls chorus

Kindergarten: "The Flag Goes By"—poem

First grade: "This Land is Your Land" by Woody Guthrie

Second grade: Poem recitation

Third grade: Poem recitation

Fourth grade: "A Tribute to Old Glory"—a reading

Fifth grade: "You're a Grand Old Flag" by George M. Cohan

Sixth grade chorus and jazz ensemble: "America"—traditional

Guest speaker: Captain Seth Williams

Recognition of veterans present: Mrs. Kennedy, principal

Taps: Handbell choir, fifth and sixth grade

Retiring of the colors

Writing

The teacher at the memorial said, "The wall is for us." Write an essay explaining her statement and how students might be affected by a visit to the wall. (English-grammar)

Social Studies

Locate the country of Vietnam. Learn some facts about Vietnam today—e.g., capital city, size, population, government, education, resources, and products. How has the country changed since it was the site of a bitter war? *Note*: Vietnam has become a major tourist attraction as well. (Social studies-maps)

Science

The wall is made of black granite. Give at least three reasons why granite was chosen for this memorial—e.g., it is hard, it can be polished, and it is impervious to weather. Have the students compare granite to other rocks—e.g., limestone, slate, marble, and sandstone. (Science-earth materials)

Mathematics

The length of the Vietnam Memorial Wall is 493.6 feet. Measure this out on the playground, having students standing at arm's length. Compare this length with other objects the students know—the gymnasium, the length of the school, a semi truck, a football field, and so on. (Math-relations)

The Arts

Many people make rubbings of the name they find. Do other rubbings of leaves, jewelry, belt buckles, coins, or any item done in relief. (Arts-media)

Computer

Search for other children's books on Vietnam by accessing online bookstores with children's departments. (English-genre)

Find information about present-day Vietnam using the Internet. Use this in conjunction with the social studies activity. (Social studies-place, Social studies-world culture)

Library Media Center

Read fictional books about Vietnam—e.g., *Journey Home* and *Angel Child, Dragon Child*. (English-genre)

Puzzle

Each number in the statement has a corresponding letter. When all the letters have been filled in, you will have an important line in the story. Use the chart in the puzzle section of *Going West* (p. 32) to assist you.

20 8 5   14 1 13 5 19   1 18 5   20 8 5   14 1 13 5 19   15 6   20 8 5

4 5 1 4.   2 21 20   20 8 5   23 1 12 12   9 19   6 15 18   1 12 12

15 6   22 19.

Answer

The names are the names of the dead. But the wall is for all of us.

REFERENCES

Frost, Helen, and Gail Saunders-Smith. *A Look at Vietnam.* Eden Prairie, MN: Pebble Books, 2002. Information on present-day Vietnam is given.

Garland, Sherry. *Children of the Dragon: Selected Tales from Vietnam.* New York: Harcourt Children's Books, 2001. These stories are suitable for reading to elementary school students.

McKay, Lawrence, Jr. *Journey Home.* New York: Lee and Low Books, 1998. Adopted by Americans, a mother goes to Vietnam to search for her birth parents.

Surat, Michele. *Angel Child, Dragon Child.* New York: Scholastic, 1989. A youngster has trouble with a fellow student until he learns about her background.

www.lonelyplanet.com/destinations/south_east_asia/vietnam. Vietnam is now regarded as a tourist attraction.

www.nps.gov/vive/memorial/memorial.htm. Information from the National Park Service describes the wall and its development.

CHAPTER 30

Celebration

Written by Jane Resch Thomas
New York: Hyperion Books for Children, 1997

SUMMARY

Keeping up with family activities is an important part of a Fourth of July celebration along with swimming and eating. Grandma is proud of her extended family that has gathered together.

RELATED CONCEPTS

celebration

feasting

RELATED VOCABULARY

station wagon	pilfer
sawhorses	bachelor
one-on-one	master of ceremonies
short leash	sparklers

ACTIVITIES

Language Arts

Which parties or celebrations are familiar to the children—Christmas, Eid, Hanukkah, Veterans Day, Chinese New Year, Saint Valentine's Day, Cinco de Mayo, graduations, and/or weddings? Allow students a short amount of time to explain each holiday or event. (Social studies-world culture)

Who generally sponsors the celebrations that the children attend—e.g., parents, the school, the church, the town, a place of employment, or an ethnic group? (Social studies-community)

Writing

The family in the book was celebrating the Fourth of July. After brainstorming what the Fourth of July means, have the students prepare a rough draft of their thoughts. Peer edit the pieces before publishing a final draft. Use these compositions as a part of a red, white, and blue bulletin board. (English-grammar)

Make a line poem about the concept of "celebration." Here are some examples. (English-grammar)

"Celebrations mean picnics."

"Celebrations mean fireworks."

Social Studies

What do we celebrate when we observe the Fourth of July? Survey a group of persons and record their answers. Do they all agree on the reasons for this celebration? (Social studies-community)

Science

Obtain a copy of the food pyramid from the Internet. Calculate a day's meals for an elementary school student. Apply this to the servings given on the pyramid. How nutritious was the meal? What changes in eating habits could be made to be more in line with the suggestions from the pyramid? (Science-health)

Mathematics

Help to plan a celebration. First, count the number of people at the party in *Celebration*. Then figure how much you will need of the following. (Math-relations)

Hot dogs and rolls	Baked beans
Macaroni salad	Chicken wings
Lemonade	Chocolate cake
Pork chops	

Make an estimate of what people will eat—e.g., five chicken wings per person, four glasses of lemonade each, and one-third pound macaroni salad. Or make a serving size—e.g., one chocolate cake serves fourteen persons. Your answer may be in pounds or in liquid measurement. Assume there are twenty-eight persons attending. (Math-relations)

The Arts

Design a float or other entry in a Fourth of July parade—e.g., a salute to our Founding Fathers, a fifth grade Civil War regiment, and women depicting the fight for women's rights. (Arts-media)

Computer

Obtain a copy of the food pyramid to use with the science activity. Are there differences between pyramids? (English-sources)

Library Media Center

Using Web sites related to the topic of food, locate recipes that would be appropriate for a picnic. How many people does the item feed? How would this be changed to have enough food for the class? (English-sources)

Puzzle

The following words are used in the exercise below:

graduation	Halloween
Eid	Labor Day
Cinco de Mayo	Diwali
Valentine's Day	Hanukkah
New Year's Day	Christmas
anniversary	New Year's Day
Memorial Day	Memorial Day

The above words match with the following descriptions:

The end of Ramadan	Ghosts, goblins, and treats
To honor workers	A commencement from school studies
The coming of the Lord	A commemoration of another year
Mexican Independence Day	To tell people you like them
The Hindu festival of lights	The start of a new calendar year
A candle is lit each night for a week	To decorate the graves of the dead

Answers

The end of Ramadan—Eid	Ghosts, goblins, and treats—Halloween
To honor workers—Labor Day	A commencement from school studies—graduation
The coming of the Lord—Christmas	A commemoration of another year—anniversary

Mexican Independence Day—Cinco de Mayo

To tell people you like them—Valentine's Day

The Hindu festival of lights—Diwali

To decorate the graves of the dead—Memorial Day

A candle is lit each night for a week—Hanukkah

The start of a new calendar year—New Year's Day

REFERENCES

Wong, Janet S. *Apple Pie Fourth of July*. New York: Harcourt Children's Books, 2002. A Chinese American girl wonders why her parents cook chow mein on the Fourth of July.

http://chinesefood.about.com/library/weekly/aa113098.htm. A factual Web site that gives information about chow mein and how it was developed by immigrants.

http://southernfood.about.com/library/weekly/aa082298.htm. Mrs. Fisher, an African American woman, is said to have published the first cookbook of African American recipes.

www.davidscooking.com/recipes/thewings/vietwings.html. This site gives a recipe for Vietnamese chicken wings.

Answers to
Crossword Puzzles

James Towne: Struggle for Survival

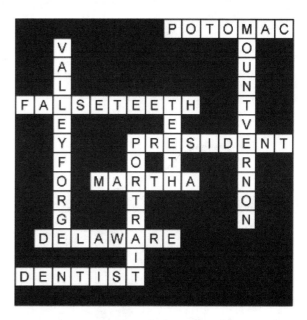

George Washington's Teeth

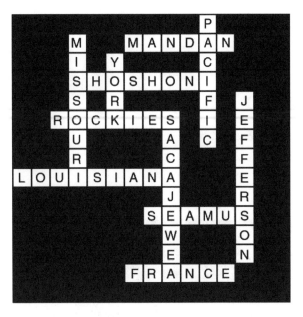

How We Crossed the West:
The Adventures of Lewis and Clark

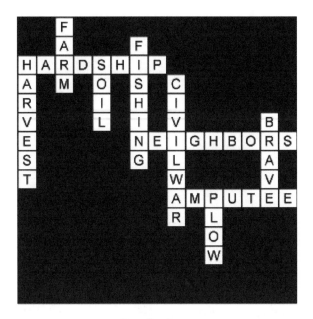

Cecil's Story

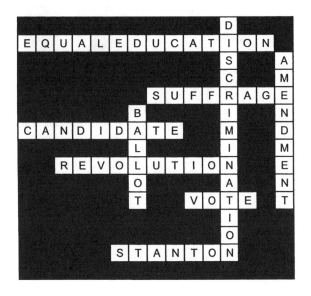

The Ballot Box Battle

Clara Barton

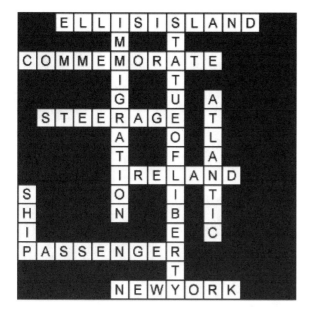

Dreaming of America

John Henry

Snowflake Bentley

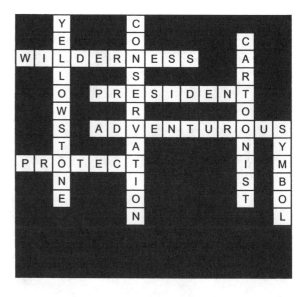

The Legend of the Teddy Bear

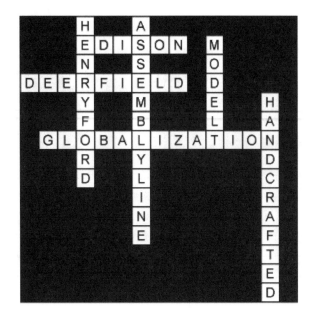

Wheels in Time

Alice Ramsey's Grand Adventure

The Gardener

Amelia and Eleanor Go for a Ride

*A Picture Book of Dwight
David Eisenhower*

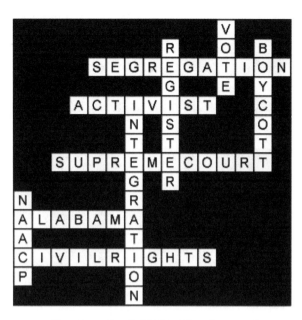

*If a Bus Could Talk: The Story of
Rosa Parks*

Grandma's Records

*Wilma Unlimited: How Wilma Rudolph
Became the World's Fastest Woman*

Harvesting Hope: The Story of
Cesar Chavez

Oh, the Places He Went

Index

About the Authors

Carol and John Butzow live in Indiana, Pennsylvania, where John is an administrator at Indiana University of Pennsylvania. Carol teaches English as a second language to elementary students. For fifteen years, they have collaborated on well-known books for teachers, including *Science through Children's Literature, The World of Work through Children's Literature, Exploring the Environment through Children's Literature*, and other titles.

John and Carol have traveled extensively throughout the United States, including Alaska, to present workshops, in-service courses, and conferences. They have also spoken to audiences in Canada, Scotland, and Sweden. For information on workshops or conferences, please contact them through Libraries Unlimited.